From Tragedy
to Triumph

A Journey

Donna,

Thanks for your interest in my
book!

I hope my book encourages and
challenges you to delve deeper
in the faith.

Acts 17:11

Love, Ryan Krafft

By Ryan J. Krafft

MW00398136

The Scripture quotations used from the following versions fall within the gratis guidelines[1] for permitted use, without express written permission from the publisher:

Scripture quotations marked (NIV) are taken from the Holy Bible, New International Version®, NIV®. Copyright © 1973, 1978, 1984, by Biblica, Inc.™ Used by permission of Zondervan. All rights reserved worldwide. www.zondervan.com The "NIV" and "New International Version" are trademarks registered in the United States Patent and Trademark Office by Biblica, Inc.™

Scripture quotations marked (NKJV) are taken from the New King James Version®. Copyright © 1982 by Thomas Nelson. Used by permission. All rights reserved.

Scripture quotations marked (ESV) are taken from the Holy Bible, English Standard Version, copyright © 2001 by Crossway Bibles, a publishing ministry of Good News Publishers. Used by permission. All rights reserved.

Scripture quotations marked (WEB) are taken from the World English Bible. Public domain.

About the Author: Ryan J. Krafft is a public speaker, sharing his personal testimony and urging people to consider the possible consequences of their decisions, as well as the effect those decisions may have on others. He is a worshiper of God and an avid student of the Bible. He holds an Associate's degree in Liberal Arts from St. Clair County Community College, as well as a Bachelor's of Arts in Psychology from the University of Michigan. He also maintains the website www.ryankrafftproject.com, where he witnesses by sharing his story and periodically updating readers on his life happenings.

Contents

Contents Continued

Written in loving memory of
Geoffrey Harris 7/8/1981 – 7/26/1998
&

Breanna Marie St.Onge 5/4/1981 – 6/30/2000

Acknowledgments

I need to recognize and thank my good friend Jill Oosterbaan for her wise textual contributions and for applying her editing skills to the manuscript copy of this book. If you notice any typos, punctuation, or grammatical problems, you should have seen it before Jill got a hold of it!

I also need to recognize and thank my friend and neighbor Marcia Collins for proofreading one of the original copies of this book and cleaning it up even more. Indeed, this was a process!

Finally, I need to recognize and thank my friend Dr. Todd Baker for checking my basic theology. Todd is president of B'rit Hadashah Ministries (www.brit-hadashah.org) and Pastor of Shalom, Shalom Messianic Congregation in Dallas, Texas. He holds a Bachelor of Science Degree in biblical studies, a Master of Theology Degree from Dallas Theological Seminary as well a Ph.D. in Philosophy and Apologetics from Trinity Seminary.

Introduction

I AM SITTING in my power chair, with my laptop computer in front of me, and a worn pencil firmly grasped between the index and middle finger of my right hand. The pencil has never been sharpened. I am not writing, I'm typing. I use the pencil backwards. I punch keys with the white eraser. My word prediction software, WordQ, assists me.

I write at the encouragement of many, and though my writing contains much of my journey, this story is not about me. This is not a memoir or an autobiography. Mine is a simple story of a prodigal, and his journey to the Father. Using my story, I hope to engage you, to encourage you in your journey, or if you have yet to step out, to call you out. As you are called out, it becomes your personal responsibility to respond.

In a recent conversation I remarked that it's too bad I'm not the journaling type. I never consistently kept a journal of any kind until I started writing this book, so many of the lessons I've learned through certain experiences will be left untold. They are misplaced in the shadows of my mind, for me to retrieve in time of need. Thankfully, my mom did keep a journal during the immediate aftermath of the crash through to my last day at the rehabilitation hospital. So I have gleaned a lot of relevant information from it. (Note: I have opted to use the word crash, rather than accident, throughout this book. When there is a car wreck involving alcohol, crash is the proper terminology.)

Having grown used to writing papers for college professors, I have a habit of wanting to use large words. I feel that there is a certain eloquence or finesse that ought to be conveyed with the written word. But such eloquence is wasted when the reader doesn't understand what he or she is reading. Therefore, I have attempted to walk a line, trying to write to be understood by most, while not sacrificing eloquence. Although at times I have also used slang terms, and this may come off as most ineloquent. So be it.

For the sake of clarity, I've made use of common literary devices throughout. I use these devices to define, clarify and explain; i.e. comes from the Latin "id est," and it means "that is." e.g. comes from the Latin "exempli gratia," and it means "for example." I prefer to think of e.g. as meaning "example given." In fact, before researching the device, I thought that that was the meaning. Finally, cf. is an abbreviation for the Latin word "confer," and it means just that, to "confer" or "compare." I use this to inform you that similar information is found elsewhere, a reference. I generally use an ellipsis (…) in quotes where I feel that the quote in its entirety is not relevant.

Also, I have divided this book into sections, rather than chapters. This is because it seemed that some areas were too short to rightly be called chapters, while others are much longer. Basically, there isn't much consistency in the length of the sections. At any rate, this is the first time I've written at length, intent on sharing with others.

Who I Was

"There is a way that seems right to a man, but in the end it leads to death."
(Proverbs 14:12 NIV)

AS I SEEK to escort you along my journey, it is essential that you understand how I became who I was, before we make a transition to who I now am. I've grown up and lived in Port Huron, Michigan all my life. But the story should start from the beginning, since there is a slight irony here. I was born into this world at St. Joe's Hospital in Sarnia, Ontario Canada on November 23rd, 1978. It was Thanksgiving that year. It's no big story as to why I was born in Sarnia. My mom simply had a bad experience with the doctors in Port Huron, so she opted for a different venue. Mom jokes that while people were eating turkey she was having one. I was her Butterball!

My parents, Jim and Ruth, raised us kids the best they knew how. They took us to St. Stephen's Catholic Church and Sunday School every week, they stayed together through hard times for us, and they instilled a good work ethic in us. I had held some kind of job since I was 13. I have two older sisters, Laurie and Nicole, who are both outgoing, so I was always the timid one.

Being shy, I always had difficulty making friends. Adolescence is a time during which most of us struggle to find an identity. In

1

intermediate school, I really only had two friends – Jeff and Nick. Although I had athletic ability, I was never confident in my ability. I guess that comes with being shy. I wasn't very involved in organized sports, however I played AYSO soccer. So I wasn't a jock, and had no desire to be one, because many in that crowd struck me as arrogant. Though I had the intellectual ability, I held As and Bs throughout high school and had I applied myself, could've easily gotten straight As, I wasn't a geek. I wasn't a freak. Who was I?

When I started high school, I saw less of my two friends, and desiring to be accepted, quickly ascertained that an easy way to be accepted into a certain crowd was through drug use. So it started. I began smoking marijuana in social circles. My inhibitions were slightly eased and I started making new friends. I became sexually promiscuous. Cheating, lying, and stealing became easier, as I had all but severed my conscience.

I was working, going to school and looking for the next party. In an effort to gain acceptance, I compromised all of my values. I was constantly listening to explicit music, trying to silence what was left of my conscience. I became *"hardened by the deceitfulness of sin."* (*Hebrews 3:13 NIV*) My friends tagged me with Kraffty for a nickname. Through a series of poor choices, I formed an identity. As shallow as it was, I was a partier. But something was missing. Inside I was empty, lonely, restless and insecure. These feelings led to thoughts of suicide and now I was on a path to self-destruction! On more than one occasion, I complained to my parents that I was bored with life...

In the following, I don't want it to sound as if my life revolved around drugs and alcohol; it didn't, or that these were the only sources of my destruction, they weren't. Other things contributed as well such as sex, pornography, explicit music, and ultimately the responsibility lies with me, but bad company was also a factor. *"Do not be misled; bad company corrupts good character." (1 Corinthians 15:33 NIV)* I became bad company myself. My peers and I were not a good influence on each other. Some of the previously mentioned activities may seem harmless to you, but just because we have become desensitized by a society that tends to trivialize such things, doesn't make them harmless.

I entered through the gateway of marijuana, and that led to other drug use and abuse. Hallucinogens, such as LSD, magic mushrooms and mescaline were viewed as only a small step past that gateway, so tripping on the weekends was not unusual. And of course, underage drinking was a norm. About a month after I graduated high school in 1997, I was busted with a quarter pound of marijuana, and charged with possession of marijuana with intent to distribute. This was a felony charge. Fortunately, the judge took into account my age and lack of a prior arrest record, and I was given HYTA status. HYTA status (Holmes Youthful Trainee Act) essentially stated that if I completed the requirements of my probation, there would be no conviction record of the crime. While on probation I was required to take urine tests once a month to prove that I was clean. I quit smoking marijuana, which left a deeper void and a more dire restlessness. Rather than try to ascertain the true cause of this condition, which I now recognize as a consequence of the Fall – separation from God, I ultimately sought to fill the void with another substance; cocaine.

The transition to cocaine use wasn't immediate. I was going to St. Clair County Community College, studying to become a mechanical engineer. I was taking courses like chemistry and calculus as well as getting prerequisites out of the way. I didn't use during the first semester, nor around new years of 1998, so I must have started sometime in late February or early March. My parents had no good reason to suspect that I had upped the ante and was now playing a more dangerous, even deadly game. I was going to college full time, earning As, Bs, and Cs, working 40+ hours a week, and hanging out with my friends. I wasn't at home very often, except to sleep, shower and change my clothes. Approximately two weeks before the crash, my mom warned me to slow down. I replied with an arrogant sense of invincibility, "Don't worry about me Mom, nothing's going to happen to me." They talk about famous last words; those very well could have been mine...

Now by the revelation of my cocaine use, I don't want to implicate any of my friends. Most of them did not use. By this time, I was hanging out with several different cliques, which I had for the most part managed to keep separate from one another. I had my group of friends that I would bring around my house and introduce to my parents, as well as a few other groups, whom I knew my parents would not approve of, so I kept them away. It's funny because my sister Laurie swore that the group of friends she used to see me hanging around with on Michigan Road, was a gang. But those were the "approved" friends. Though several of my friends were in gangs, I would never join one because I had friends in rival gangs. Besides, I already had a real family.

Being 19, and of legal drinking age in Canada, I went over with my friends to party quite often. Now this very act was criminal, since one of the stipulations of my probation was that I was not to leave the state of Michigan, let alone the country!

I was steady living on the edge and it was bound to catch up with me. In the spring and summer of 1998, everything came to a nasty head.

In early April, a good friend of mine died of a drug overdose. Knowing that cocaine had been a contributing factor, I tried to quit. But I couldn't. The feelings of emptiness, loneliness, restlessness, and insecurity returned with a vengeance. The white demon that possessed me was flexing its muscle. As a result of my friend's death, I was unable to snort with my usual clique. It wasn't right and now we knew it. We were stripped of all excuses! Since I was unable to quit, I shifted cliques to one who knew of my friend, but was farther removed.

Sometime that spring, I met a wonderful young lady named Brea. If she had known about the junk I was involved with, she would have intervened I'm sure. But I kept our relationship away from most of my friends and her in the dark, away from all that was destroying me.

Backtracking a bit. After graduation, my dad sold me his 1990 Ford Ranger pick-up truck for $1,000. The truck was in mint condition! I installed a box with a pair of 12" subwoofers and an amplifier in the extended cab. Yeah, I was that obnoxious kid with the bass thumping that you could hear coming from a half mile away. In early July, I took my bravado to the next level! I pimped out the truck with low profile tires and some tight rims. That truck was my most prized possession. It was my god! Any spare cash I could round up, besides supporting my addictions, went into that truck.

My friends and I were really into a Detroit based rap group called Natas (read that backwards). The group consisted of three members; Esham, who referred to himself as "The Unholy", Mastamind and TNT. In hindsight, the music seems very juvenile, but at the time we all thought it was cool. With albums such as Boomin Words From Hell, KKKill the Fetus, Closed Casket, Blaz4me, Doubelieveingod, and Multikillionaire; (The Devils

5

Contract), it should be clear what they were about. Their music mocked God and glorified evil. Whether or not they even bought into the garbage they preached is irrelevant; they had a following. Why is this important? Because not too long before the crash, I had their record company's logo tattooed on my back; the devil in the moon.

I listened to a lot of different rap artists such as Master P, C-Murder, The Notorious B.I.G., Too $hort, and others. I also listened to metal groups like; Pantera, White Zombie, Tool, Type O Negative, Megadeth, KoRn, and others, but nothing as overtly evil as Esham and Natas. However, I will say that their overtly satanic message was less deceitful than others – at least you knew what you were getting into.

I was rolling high! But the stage was set. I had pushed it to the limits. Something bad was about to happen.

The Crash

"Pride goes before destruction and a haughty spirit before a fall." (Proverbs 16:18 NKJV)

"Some became fools through their rebellious ways and suffered affliction because of their iniquities." (Psalm 107:17 NIV)

AFTER BEING IN a coma for just under a month, I awoke in St. Mary's Hospital in Saginaw, Michigan. I couldn't move, I couldn't speak, and a machine that helped me breathe was hooked up to a tube in my trachea (windpipe). I was trapped in a prison of my own making!

I cannot remember most of the week before the crash, let alone the crash itself. So, what had happened? I couldn't communicate, so the question just hung there, like a hammer – ready to drop.

Here's what happened; on July 26, 1998, after partying at a bar in Sarnia, Canada, I headed home after 2 AM. While turning left at an intersection, traveling approximately 15 mph, I was broadsided or t-boned by a 1-ton pickup truck, a Ford F-350 going approximately 65 mph in a 30 mph zone. Did I run the red light? Or did they? We'll never know. It doesn't matter anyway, knowing wouldn't change anything. Besides, I wasn't supposed to be there in the first place.

In the crash, I was presumably tossed through the window of my truck, and directly into a coma. I was immediately taken to Sarnia General Hospital, where they weren't equipped to handle a trauma victim. Apparently, it was very foggy that morning, and there were many other accidents. Since the trauma units in Michigan were unable to take me, I was flown by helicopter to Queen Victoria Hospital in London, Ontario.

In London, they installed a feeding tube, a catheter, and a titanium rod in my right leg to hold the bone in alignment, because my tibia (i.e. shin bone) was broken. They repaired my diaphragm, removed my spleen and performed a tracheotomy. A tracheotomy is when a hole is cut in the windpipe to help with breathing, and a tube is inserted in the hole and hooked to oxygen. These were the medical and surgical procedures used to repair my body and sustain my life. Beyond this, I had broken ribs, a broken collar bone, and a lacerated liver. On several occasions, I was dangerously close to death. At one point my temperature was 106.8.

The Canadian doctors gave my parents very grave reports. Initially, in Sarnia, they thought my back was broken and when they did a CT scan in London, they reported only slight brain activity, hinting that I might be in a vegetative state. They gathered a team of doctors, nurses and a psychologist and presented, or rather pressured my parents with the option of pulling the plug, asking, "Would Ryan want to live like this?" My parents prayed and talked about it and decided that if God allowed me to live, they would take me in whatever condition He gave.

When I was stable enough, a day past the two-week mark, they flew me to St. Mary's Hospital in Saginaw, Michigan. My dad flew with me and my mom went home. When I arrived, I was no longer stable. My dad had to call my mom and tell her to rush to Saginaw that evening because I wasn't expected to live. My oldest sister Laurie drove my mom up to Saginaw, where they stayed the night. The next day, the doctors said that I was stable, and they were just going to do some x-rays. So my mom and Dad drove back down to Port Huron with my sister to ensure her safe arrival and to grab some clothes, food, showers, etc. Meanwhile, back in Saginaw, the x-rays revealed that I had blood clots in my legs, heading for my lungs and heart. My parents arrived home to a message on the answering machine, informing them of the situation and that they needed to okay surgery. They called, "okayed" the surgery, then turned around and quickly headed back up to Saginaw. Food, clothes and showers were now unimportant.

The operation they performed is referred to as a vena cava interruption. This is the placement of a filter in the inferior vena cava, to trap blood clots and prevent clots in the lungs and heart. The inferior vena cava is the large vein that returns deoxygenated blood to the heart. It is located in the lower abdomen. The filter they put into me is called a Greenfield Filter. So now I have this wicked, twisted, upside down umbrella-looking device resting in my abdomen.

Thankfully, my neurologist, Dr. Malcolm Fields, gave my parents a much more optimistic report than the Canadians had. My back was not broken and the CT scan showed very noticeable brain activity. Dr. Fields told my parents that if I did wake up, my intellect would be slightly diminished. He said that if I was an A/B student, I would now be a B/C student.

My parents stayed in a motor home they owned, which St. Mary's allowed them to park in the parking lot. This allowed them to stay close to me. From my understanding, they rarely left.

Finally, after 23 days in a coma, on August 17th, I awoke. Ironically, it was my parents' 24th wedding anniversary. My mom wrote in her journal; *"Our 24th anniversary. We told Ryan all we wanted was for him to open his eyes and get better."* My dad went home for a cardiology appointment that he was supposed to have the next day. My mom went to her cousin Lydia's house, which was close by, so that she could take a shower and spend the night there while my dad was away. Later that evening she called to see which nurses were working. The nurse on duty informed my mom that I was restless and thrashing. She asked my mom if she could give me some pain medication, and my mom gave the go ahead.

She didn't feel comfortable staying away, so she and Lydia headed back up to the hospital. At approximately 11:00 PM, when she walked in, the nurse was talking to me. Seeing my mom, she asked me to blink three times if I recognized her. I did. After the many negative predictions by the Canadian doctors, the fact that I was awake and recognized her, overwhelmed my mom with tears of joy. She then called my dad, who said that he was afraid to answer the phone. When he finally answered and heard the crying, he assumed that they'd lost me. Needless to say, he was very relieved when he heard the news.

I could have been completely paralyzed for all I knew. I couldn't move or even make a sound. I couldn't eat or drink, except through the tube lodged in my stomach. There I lay, with a machine pumping oxygen into my lungs, sustaining my life. Eventually, I ascertained the answer to my question. I had suffered a Traumatic Brain Injury (TBI) as a result of a car crash. Later I would learn more – like when, where and how.

I was by no means "out of the woods." I contended with infections, pneumonias and congestion in my lungs. My mom wrote about the pain she saw in my face, eyes full of tears and of how tired I was. In her journal my mom wrote, *"Ryan uncomfortable, I think he realizes he can't do things and he is depressed."*

I learned to express my emotions even within the limited ability I had at my disposal. I would hold my breath and keep my eyes closed. Obviously, holding my breath didn't last long, but apparently I would go for days without opening my eyes. Dr. Fields had been encouraging my parents to find a rehabilitation hospital. My mom wrote, *"Went to Ann Arbor, Southfield, and Lapeer – decision; Hurley Hospital (Flint). Ryan showed us he is angry we left him so long, wouldn't look at us."*

On September 16th, 1998, I was moved by ambulance to Hurley Hospital in Flint, Michigan. I remember thinking that I wasn't going to make it. My lungs were filling up with phlegm and I had broken out in a terrible cold sweat. The first night there was pure hell. At St. Mary's they would shoot me up with painkillers as needed. At Hurley, there was a certain male nurse, who boasted that he was a marine medic, and he said that I would have to "suck it up." He offered Tylenol, which after having powerful painkillers when needed, didn't ease my pain one iota. Later on, a nice black nurse named Ruthie, hooked me up with the much needed pain killers. But before Ruthie arrived, my lungs were filling up with phlegm again. When this happened they would take a suction hose, stick it in my trachea and into my lungs, in order to withdraw the phlegm. They did this at St. Mary's also, but that first night at Hurley, this male nurse did it so violently that rather than give me the much-needed relief, it caused me further pain. We got the impression it was because we had 'bothered' him.

My parents were beginning to wonder if they had made the right choice. They stayed with me that night, and lodged a complaint against that nurse. I only saw him working that floor one other time. Thank God he was the exception! Eventually, my parents were able to rent an apartment across the street from the hospital. I hated it when they left me, but I knew they had to.

On September 22nd they removed my trach tube. I was able to breathe on my own now. I was hit with this realization; "baby steps… I'm in for a long war!"

The next day I met my therapists. For physical therapy, there was Dee, an attractive petite lady with tanned skin and dark hair. Peter was doing his internship at Hurley and he was very helpful during this time. Peter was a self-described "tall skinny white guy." Shortly after Peter finished his internship, Dee let another therapist work with me in her stead. Melissa was a gorgeous brunette with a beautiful smile, whom I had a crush on. So needless to say, I looked forward to physical therapy a bit more now! My occupational therapy, with Sue, whom I had nicknamed "the pain lady", and speech therapy with Stacy, increased in difficulty. My dad did range of motion with me, moving all my limbs. I was unable to sleep well, being fortunate to get 3 hours, which made it difficult to do therapy during the day.

I couldn't speak and I was unable to use the call button. Fortunately, my room was directly across from the nurses' station and I had learned how to scream. Not manly screams, but a high-pitched shrill shriek, which I could maintain for a few seconds before running out of breath. I was accused by more than one nurse of sounding like a cat in heat.

For a while I had to have heparin shots in my stomach three times a day. Heparin is a blood thinner, which is used to prevent blood clots. Over time, my stomach took on the look of an old banana; bruises surrounded by yellow. The shots didn't bother me and seldom hurt. Still, the nurses would always relay their remorse at having to give the shots. I'd just smile, to let them know it was okay.

In Canada they put in a certain kind of feeding tube, known as a J-tube. The J-tube went directly to my lower bowel and it was hooked to a pump that ensured slow feeding. Because of its cumbersome nature, it had been accidentally pulled out during physical therapy. My rehab doctor, Alpiner, made an appointment for me to get a G-tube, which would go to my stomach and require periodic feedings, thus separating me from the pump.

Dr. Alpiner requested a certain kind of G-tube. It was a button that was flush with my skin and would have given me more freedom during therapy. The doctor who performed this procedure froze my throat and put me under anesthesia. He then used an endoscope, which he put down my throat into my stomach in order to locate the stomach. He didn't have the right size button. What he had was too small, but he put it in anyway.

Later that night, after the procedure, I wasn't feeling so hot. My favorite night time nurse, Barb, was sitting with me when I began to vomit. She turned my head and grabbed a basin. Thank God she was there. Otherwise I might have choked to death on my own vomit.

After a couple of days, the small button that the doctor had inserted became infected, so it had to be removed. They didn't freeze the area, put me out or anything. Dr. Alpiner just grabbed a hold of this thing and started pulling until it came out. My mom left the room. I wish I could have left as well! At the end of the button was a plastic ball, called a retention dome. It was about the size of a nickel in circumference. Anyway, Dr. Alpiner just pulled this thing through the small hole that was already there. I didn't scream or anything, but talk about pain! That was probably the most intense pain I'd ever felt. Needless to say, the small hole was no longer small.

They put an N.G.-tube in while the wound healed. An N.G.-tube, or nasogastric tube, is the typical temporary kind that we're used to seeing. They shove the tube through your nostrils, down your esophagus, while you slowly gag on it, into your stomach. Then they hook that to a pump. A week or so later, after the wound healed, I was sent back down to the same doctor who did me up so great before. I was afraid that I wouldn't make it through the night.

It wasn't the procedure that scared me so much, but how I felt afterward was still fresh in my mind. And Barb wasn't working that night! Much to my relief, everything went well this time. I felt fine afterward, no vomiting, and I had a feeding tube with about 9 inches of tube extending out from the entry point. The important thing was that it fit. We would take care of the extra tube by placing it in a pouch that was attached to a belt-like thing that wrapped around my waist.

Eventually, the opportunity arose to let my parents know that I had my long-term memory. My short-term capabilities had already been established in speech therapy. My dad was bemoaning the fact that he needed my social security number for something and didn't have it on him. I got his attention and he said, "No, you don't remember it! Do you?" I blinked it out to him. While I was excited to demonstrate that my long-term memory was still intact, I felt eerily like the dog *Lassie,* from the television show by that name. ("What's that Lassie? Timmy's trapped in a well!?") My dad, of course, didn't believe me, so he double checked and sure enough, I had it right. Now they knew that not only did I remember people, I remembered other things as well. It was me in this broken body.

After my mom was sure that I was cognizant, she explained to me that I had been in a drinking and driving crash, and that she wouldn't talk anymore with me about it until I was better. Everyone gave me the impression that I was alone in my truck during the crash, so that disarmed any questions I had in regard to that issue.

At some point, they weighed me. They put my wheelchair on the scale to weigh it by itself first and then put me in the chair and put me on the scale. Long before the crash, when I was 15, I had been in the habit of working out at the gym three days a week, so I was pretty physically fit – 6' tall, and approximately 180 pounds – solid. Now these scales read 123 pounds! I remember the first time I saw my full body in the mirror, I couldn't believe it was me. I mean my face looked the same, but my limbs were so scrawny.

They came up with a way for me to communicate with my eyes; an ABC chart, which took forever, but worked. I held my eyes tight until they came to the row that the letter was in, 5 rows, and then I fluttered my eyes. Down the row, until the letter, I fluttered again. They then would write the letter on a dry erase board.

Remember Brea, the young lady I wrote about earlier in "Who I Was?" Well, at the time I couldn't remember, but we split up before the crash because she caught me cheating on her. She caught me on a date with another young lady. But she stuck by me anyway. Before it happened, she had a quiet prayerful confidence that I would wake from the coma. Now that I was awake and had a way to communicate, I told her that I loved her with the blinks and the board. She then inquired if I considered her my girlfriend. I fluttered my eyes for "yes." Next, she asked if she was the only one, and again I fluttered, "yes." After that day she never returned to the hospital to visit me. I honestly didn't remember cheating on her, yet. A couple weeks later I received a letter and picture in the mail from the girl I cheated on Brea with, so my memory was jogged, and now I knew. But my foolish pride would soon best me again. In all honesty, I was actually seeing someone else when I started dating Brea. Yeah, I was a creep!

Though I believed in the existence of God, I did not yet know Him. Nevertheless, looking back I see Him at work. By bringing people into my life, who exemplified a godly, compassionate attitude, He was drawing me to Himself. Though there were many during my time at Hurley, three in particular stand out in my mind. First, my mom's cousin Tom would come up to the hospital and pray with us for my recovery. On one occasion, when Tom came to pray with us, I was in therapy, so he prayed over my bed and left a note that he was there.

When I came back from therapy, I was exhausted and wanted badly to go to bed for a nap. However, my dad liked to have me out of the bed for as long as possible, because once I got into bed, that's where I stayed for the rest of the day. So began a battle of wills. I'd look at my dad and then to the bed, indicating my desire. My dad would say "No." I swear this went on for at least 20 minutes. Finally, my mom broke the impasse; I would get to go to bed. I fell asleep almost immediately, and when I woke up, I was able to move my right leg.

Another positive influence was Terry, a tall black male nurse, who would drop in my room for occasional visits. Though I couldn't tell, he told me that he too had been in a car accident and testified to God's work in his life. One of the most difficult things for me was learning to hold my head up again; my chin would literally fall to my chest after approximately 10 seconds. One day Terry brought me in a copy of one of his Gospel albums, *Evolution of Gospel,* by The Sounds of Blackness. It had this real funky, jazzy song on it called

"Hold On (Change is Comin')." Not only were the lyrics very inspirational, but the funky beat got down into my soul and I began lifting my head off the bed, be-boppin. This did wonders for my neck strength!

The third person who stands out was an elderly black gentleman my parents and I encountered while in the lobby one day. On his way up to see somebody, stopped and said "looks like this young man needs some prayer," as he removed his hat and bowed his head to pray for me. I really took notice of these small acts of kindness and almost all of them had one factor in common – they came from Christians.

Anyway, after two months in Hurley, I was being discharged. Not because I was ready, but because I wasn't improving enough. They were giving up on me. They told my parents they should put me in a nursing home. My parents would have none of that. They were taking me home! I still had my feeding tube, so my dad learned how to use it. He had been doing the range of motion exercises with me all along.

I was so excited to be going home that the last week of my stay I started improving rapidly. Hurley's therapists took notice of this improvement and told my parents they'd like to keep me longer. But my parents were adamant. There was no way that they were getting my hopes up and then crushing them. I was excited because I would be home for my 20th birthday, my birthday being on the 23rd of November, and I was slated to go home on the 20th.

Before I left, this cute nurse came into my room. She didn't know I couldn't talk. My parents told her that I was going home for my birthday. She looked at me and asked how old I was gonna be. I blurted out clear as day "twenty." My parents looked at me and asked me to say it again. But I couldn't do it. I didn't know how I was able to do it so easily the first time. It was very strange, but a sign of good things to come.

Home

I ARRIVED HOME in the evening, after a hectic ride back from Hurley. It was Hectic for the simple fact that I was uncomfortable. I would still get cold sweats periodically, and it seemed like I had them non-stop on the ride home. Also, I had a tendency to lean off to the right. My dad called it "the Chicago lean." He had to pull off to the side of the expressway a couple of times to readjust me. And although my neck was stronger, it wasn't yet strong enough to maintain much control over my head. Fortunately, the insurance company equipped me with a tilt-in-space wheelchair with a head rest. But as the lean went, so went my head.

My parents had a wheelchair ramp built for me, and upon entering the house, I was greeted by my nephew, Colby Laurie's oldest child, who was holding a card that his first grade teacher had helped him create. It had the signatures of all his classmates inside. Also inside was a nice get well wish from his teacher, Mrs. Houston, who ironically, had also been my first grade teacher.

A few days later, I celebrated my 20th birthday. I received many presents as between 30 to 35 of my friends stopped by to visit me throughout the day. I can only imagine how I must have looked to them. I know how I felt. I could only say one or two words with little clarity, tilted back because of the difficulty with holding my head up, and I don't remember when this started happening or when it stopped, but my jaw would lock open, so I would salivate and start drooling on myself. My dad would come and put his hand on my chin to force my jaw closed.

Not only was my own life turned upside down, but so was my family's. Before the crash, the last time my sister Nicole and I had seen one another, we did not part on good terms. So after she heard about the crash, she and her husband PJ packed up with their two babies and moved back to Port Huron, from California. They lived in the basement of my parents' house while trying to start a new life in Port Huron. The crash took place the morning before my niece Chelsea's 3rd birthday, so at the time, my sister Laurie was dealing with more than she could handle. It never occurred to me that an ill-thought decision could have consequences that would be so far reaching. Fortunately, my dad had retired from Ford Motor Company six months prior to the crash, so he was able to devote most of his time to my care. My mom worked for the state of Michigan at the Family Independence Agency. After taking leave, she would soon have to return to work.

A hospital bed was parked in the living room for me. My parents would sleep out on the couch attending to me. I remember I still used my notorious "scream" to get my parents attention when I had to use the bathroom, but I now had another problem which kept them up at night. I learned to speak of this issue, which I did often. One word, "itch." Do you know what it's like to have an itch that you're unable to scratch? Well, I was unable to move, but I sure could feel. So every time I'd feel an itch, I'd voice it – "itch!" Then I had the problem of trying to communicate its whereabouts. Fortunately, it was mostly my nose that itched.

Not long after my birthday, I began to miss Brea, who didn't show on my birthday. I had my mom call her, and ask her over to see me. We had a nice visit, until she again asked me if I remembered what happened before the crash. Now this time, of course, I did remember, but a fool and his pride are not easily separated. I held fast to the tired excuse, "I don't remember." I'm not sure, but I think all she desired was an admission of guilt and an apology. When she left, I didn't know that would be the last time I'd see her.

I was set to begin my incomplete road to recovery. Before Thanksgiving, which was on the 26th of November that year, we set out to find an outpatient therapy clinic that would meet my needs. The two local clinics rejected me as a prospective patient because they felt they were not equipped to handle me. So the search continued and my parents took me to another facility about a half an hour out of town at River District Hospital in St. Clair, Michigan. We had a meeting with the therapists there and they were eager to get started with me. I would start Monday morning. In hindsight, that short journey of approximately three months, with my new therapists, was where I made the most gains. My therapists included Roseanne, a speech pathologist who was on the short side, with tanned skin, brown hair, glasses and a perfume I recognized as cigarette smoke. Sue, a physical therapist, who was about 5'9", tall for a woman, with short curly sand colored hair and Vicki, an occupational therapist of average height and size for a woman. She had brown hair that hung to her shoulders, and she wore glasses.

Sue and Vicki teamed up and began working on my trunk control. Without a core, one can't do much. Before long, they had me up on my feet walking with a walker, which was quite an ordeal. Sue sat in front of me, in a chair, helping my legs move. Vicki was behind me, helping me shift my weight. And then, of course, we needed a third individual, usually my dad, to move Sue's chair back with every step. With time, we were able to ditch the chair, and I was able to walk with just Sue behind me, helping me shift.

Meanwhile, Roseanne was working with my speech. My tongue started working, so that I was able to speak. But I lacked clarity, and it was difficult to speak in sentences, because my diaphragm had been injured, limiting my air supply. So we worked at stringing words together.

I was at River District from the end of November until approximately the middle of February. Then my physical therapist, Sue, with whom I had developed a solid relationship, decided she was going to quit the hospital and do home therapy for Beacon Home Care. So I followed. She talked the occupational therapist, Vicki, into continuing my treatment through Beacon. I had a new speech therapist, Kathy. She was a very attractive blonde, who focused on helping me regain my ability to eat, as well as continuing my speech therapy.

Nothing was instantaneous; every gain I made came with hard work and patience. Remember...baby steps! We got my tongue working enough so that I was able to swallow. But I had yet to perfect the art of chewing, so my mom would puree all kinds of things for me, including pizza. Funny, it looked disgusting, but it tasted like pizza! I remember at Hurley, the speech therapist, Stacey, asked what I'd like to eat. I indicated steak. She kind of gave me a look, like *get real*, so I quickly thought of something easy, and indicated canned peaches. Why that? I don't know, I don't even like canned peaches!

At this point, I was unable to feed myself. So, like an infant, I was donned with a bib, placed in the kitchen, and spoon fed. Eventually, I would gain enough use of my arms and hands that I was able to feed myself. I would eat at the table from now on!

I finally got my feeding tube removed almost a year after the crash, on July 13th 1999. Although I don't have an exact date for this accomplishment, I would eventually eat steak, and I continue to enjoy steak to this day!

Being Drawn

"I drew them with gentle cords, with bands of love, and I was to them as those who take the yoke from their neck. I stooped and fed them." (Hosea 11:4 NKJV)

"The LORD is near to all who call on him, to all who call on him in truth." (Psalm 145:18 ESV)

GOD HAD MY attention now. I was no longer able to ignore or reject His call, as I had done for years. Shattered were the illusions of self-sufficiency, self-reliance, and independence. Like the prodigal son of Luke 15, I had taken the blessings of God, but rejected the One from Whom the blessings flowed.

One moment of rejecting God's call stands out in my mind, most likely because of where it occurred. It happened some time before the crash, while waiting to speak to customs, on my way to party in Canada. With the music down, waiting for the car ahead of me to get through, the Lord clearly spoke to me through my conscience.

I was being called to follow Christ and being confronted with the prospect of eternal judgment for the way I was living my life. My efforts to silence my conscience were likely typical. I justified my sin by pointing to others. *"I'm not as bad as many people."* Then I threw my

"hands" up in defeat, thinking, *The whole world's going to hell anyway.*
And finally, *"I'll seize your grace and follow you when I'm old, Lord."*

I knew the way I was living was wrong and I thought that I could take advantage of God's grace when I was good and ready. I was making some dangerous presumptions! I testified earlier that I had all but severed my conscience. I experienced the reality behind this quote; "One of the most fearful things about sin is its power to harden the one who practices it. The deeper a man goes in sin, the less sin bothers him."[2] Thankfully, God was merciful to me by reviving my conscience and allowing me to taste only a fragment of the destruction I pursued, but sparing me from the totality of it. Indeed, God saved me from myself!

I had a desire to know this God Who spoke in my conscience and saved me from myself. Helping to facilitate this desire was my Christian counselor, Dave. Dave was a guy who stood about 2 inches above 6 foot, had rosy cheeks on occasion, with the beginnings of gray streaking his dark hair. He once asked me if I was angry with God. I said no, and then thought to myself, *"How can I honestly be angry with Someone I don't even know?"* I'll never understand how the most ardent atheists are so obviously angry with a deity that they supposedly don't even believe exists. People who don't believe in God ought to be indifferent towards Him, because you can't have strong feelings towards Someone who you don't believe exists.

Though I had always believed in the Triune God and knew enough about Him that I was convicted of my sinful lifestyle, I never knew God. That is, I never entered into a personal relationship with Him. I never entertained any illusions that God was under any obligation to protect me. Even with my limited understanding, I knew that I was living in full-blown rebellion against Him.

26

Another witness in my life, who was probably the greatest influence, was a nurse's aide I had, Tresa. Tresa was a wife and mother of two, with short brown hair and of average size and height for a woman. I saw her 5 days a week. While helping attend to my physical needs, she was subtly speaking to my spiritual needs as well. There were obviously other influencers in my life, but Tresa and my Christian counselor, Dave, stand out as the most prominent.

Even though I had grown up in a church and always had an interest in spiritual realities – that is to say that while I had a propensity toward things pertaining to faith – I did not enter into Christianity lightly or blindly. I did not check my intelligence at the door of faith, as Christianity is not merely a life changing faith, (which I had yet to embrace), but also a verifiably evidentially reasonable faith. Rather than be diminished, my intellect was sharpened as I researched the claims of Christ. Contrary to popular belief, faith is not a blind leap. Rather it is a proper response to evidence.

The only Bible I had was a King James Version (KJV), with that old school-language that tripped me up when I was younger. Because of this, I had a predisposed distaste for the KJV and I had no idea that there were other versions available until Tresa told me about a Family Christian bookstore in town. There I picked up the popular New International Version (NIV), which I recommend for beginners. I didn't bother asking anyone where to begin. I just assumed as with any other book I'd ever read I should begin at the beginning, Genesis. But I encourage you to start with the Gospel according to John in the New Testament, and then read Paul's letter to the Romans. However, the Old Testament is the foundation of New Testament scripture, so I am not suggesting that you neglect the Old Testament. I simply don't think it's the best place to start.

As an aside; I now prefer reading the New King James Version (NKJV), simply because there is a beauty displayed in this translation that isn't in the NIV. For me it was like moving from high school reading to college level, without the distaste referred to above. In the original manuscript of this book, most of the Scripture quotes came from the NIV. However, I became aware that as an author, you are only permitted to quote a certain amount of Scriptures from any one version, before you have to obtain written permission from the publisher of that version. So in order to avoid the process of seeking permission, I have decided to use several different versions.

Interestingly, when I first began to read the Bible, I noticed that I had some vision problems. I had to get real close to the text in order to read. Therefore, my mom scheduled me for an appointment with an optometrist (an eye doctor). I returned from the appointment with the understanding that I was nearsighted, so glasses were prescribed. My vision wasn't terrible, as it only affected my ability to read.

With glasses on, I returned to reading the Bible. Within a couple of months, I noticed myself looking under the glasses. Now the glasses were impeding my ability to read.

I returned to the optometrist and he confirmed that my 20/20 vision had been restored. He suggested that some swelling may have gone down from the head trauma, causing my vision to return to normal. I'm not implying that a miracle took place, but a blessing, that I didn't ask for, nor would have ever thought to. To say the least, this experience provided me with an analogy of how, while reading the Bible, my spiritual vision began to clarify as well.

After much reading, I arrived in the New Testament. As I was reading the Gospels with an open heart, I was convinced that Jesus was and is the Messiah (i.e. Christ), Savior and God. But I didn't really know what to do, that is, how to apply it to myself. *"But as many as received him, to them he gave the right to become God's children, to those who believe in his name: who were born not of blood, nor of the will of the flesh, nor of the will of man, but of God." (John 1:12-13 WEB)*

At some point, while lying in bed watching TV, I came across a televangelist who was inviting the viewers to pray to receive the Lord. With the knowledge acquired from my studies, I prayed with him out of my need, out of my brokenness, out of what was seemingly a hopeless situation. I didn't try to make any deals with God, I just came before Him as I was; hurt, broken and rejected. Though, I'll be the first one to admit that the main reason I accepted Jesus as Lord was in hopes of physical healing, as I had read much about the miracles He performed!

What I didn't realize at the time, was that in that moment, the Lord had in fact performed a miracle. Spiritual life was birthed within, as God was drawing me into a relationship with Himself. Reflecting back to the story of the prodigal son found in Luke 15:11-32, the Father, though I had hardly known Him, ran to me! I suddenly had this desire to know God more than ever, and as a result I had an insatiable hunger for His Word! It came alive and I enjoyed it with a growing understanding, as though scales had fallen from my eyes! (cf. Acts 9:18) In my seemingly hopeless situation, I now had an eternal and living hope!

Throughout this time of being drawn and beyond, I experienced much doubt, and to say that it ended after I received Jesus as my Lord and Savior would be insincere. Faith that is not tested in the crucible of doubt will remain shallow. That is not to say we should seek to have our faith tested by doubt, but rather, if we have faith, its testing is inevitable. This inevitable testing most often comes down to the veracity of the Bible. Unbelievers know that if they can discredit the Bible, then doubt will be cast on Christianity as well.

Skeptics are fond of pointing out alleged errors and contradictions in the Bible, even using their own perception of morality to accuse God of immoral acts. Such assertions have caused many who once professed faith in Christ to fall away (cf. Matthew 13:20-21). No doubt, there are difficult passages and verses that appear to contradict each other. However, it must be recognized that a difference is not a contradiction. Differences can be reconciled, while contradictions cannot. If one can give a reasonable explanation of the text containing the alleged contradiction, the claim of contradiction falls apart.

In truth, scholars have pored over these texts for centuries and have concluded that no true contradictions exist. They have reconciled every text. Most claims of biblical contradictions stem from the reader misunderstanding or misrepresenting the author's intent, thereby misinterpreting the passage or verse in question.

Concerning alleged immoral acts that were committed or commanded by God, the skeptic reveals a bias that leads to a gross misunderstanding of the character God as revealed in the Bible. Those who assert such things do not understand the Holy nature of God. They also fail to take contextual considerations into account that reveal the foreknowledge (cf. Genesis 15:16) and patience (cf. 2 Peter 3:9) of God, before He executes judgment. They do not understand or regard the vile rituals performed for foreign gods (cf. Deuteronomy 12:31) or the contaminating nature of this sin (cf. Judges 3:6).

Therefore, I've learned not be intimidated because the Bible and the Christian faith have withstood nearly two millennia of attacks. They are trustworthy! Indeed, Christianity is one of the only religions that invites skeptics to examine the evidence of its authenticity, and no matter what is claimed, nobody rejects Christianity for lack of evidence. "The skeptic rejects Jesus Christ out of personal prejudice rather than from thorough and unbiased investigation and evidence."[3]

While most authors place their overviews in the introduction, I have chosen to place a partial overview here. I have done this because you'll notice a change in the focus of my writing. I have woven my personal journey throughout, as I seek to introduce you to the Savior. I intend to do this by showing the universal need for a Savior in **Bad News in the Mirror,** as well as elaborating on what is known as "the fall of man" in **The Real Tragedy. In A Time of Darkness,** I share my experience of being confronted with the holiness of God after a time of silence and perceived abandonment by Him. In **The Beginning of Romance,** I show that God's heart is for you, that He pursues you. In **The Real Triumph,** I explain the Gospel and introduce a few relevant concepts to help you better understand the Gospel. In **Basics,** I present some principles that are basic and essential to biblical Christianity. In **An Assault on Pride by Faith,** I explain how to apply the Gospel to your life. I also describe the effect grace has on pride. In **Of Great Consequence,** I discuss the eternal consequences of rejecting the Gospel. In **Who I am,** I describe how I came to understand who I am in Christ. In **Becoming,** I talk about how we are called to participate with God in becoming who we are in Christ. In **Deception,** I explain how deception abounds, and as foretold in the Bible, is leading to a great departure from the Christian faith. In **War,** I explain how I went through an intense struggle in the spiritual realm. In **Knowing the Enemy,** I do some unmasking of our adversary.

Bad News in the Mirror

"Rules are beautiful because they tell you you're breaking something.
Without the law, there is no knowledge of sin – and without
knowledge of sin there's no salvation from sin. That is pretty simple
and I have a definition of sin that's pretty encompassing – anything
that causes God pain." (No Compromise: The Keith Green Story;
Melody Green and David Hazard)[1]

THERE ARE MANY reasons why people reject the Gospel, but
I believe that the most prominent reason comes down to pride
and a failure to recognize sin as sin. Thus, my sister Laurie and I
have a disagreement. She asserts that most people reject the Gospel
because they don't think God will forgive them for their sins, while I
maintain that most people don't even realize they need to be
forgiven. Granted, there are people who recognize their sin and it is
so heinous that they don't believe they can be forgiven. But it is my
contention that the majority don't recognize sin for what it is.

Just as there are physical laws that regulate the universe, there are
spiritual laws which regulate the soul. Our problem is most of us
don't recognize the *gravity* of our sins. I contend that we have
become so desensitized to sin that we have deceived ourselves into
believing we are healthy, when in fact, sin is the disease that's killing
us all! Worse than that, according to Scripture, apart from Christ, we

are dead (cf. Ephesians 2:1; Colossians 2:13). That is, we have no spiritual life within us. We are separated from God.

In this section and the next, I hope to cut straight to the core of your soul, through to your conscience, and show you just how messed up we are. I have heard people assert time and time again, "I'm a good person," and when asked why God should allow them into heaven, they appeal to their own goodness. "Because I'm a good person." But how do you measure your goodness? If you're like I used to be, you measure your own goodness by comparing yourself to other people whom you perceive to be worse than you. Now by this standard, you may be good in a general sense. And this is the sense that most people mean when they refer to goodness. But when you throw God in the mix (ultimate goodness), while still measuring yourself by this standard, you are bringing God down to your standard, rather than measuring yourself by His standard. You are in effect trying to establish your own righteousness. You are playing the Pharisee.

"To some who were confident of their own righteousness (In the ultimate sense, righteousness is the state of moral perfection required by God to enter heaven) *and looked down on everybody else, Jesus told this parable: "Two men went up to the temple to pray, one a Pharisee and the other a tax collector. The Pharisee stood up and prayed about himself: 'God, I thank you that I am not like other men—robbers, evildoers, adulterers—or even like this tax collector. I fast twice a week and give a tenth of all I get.' "But the tax collector stood at a distance. He would not even look up to heaven, but beat his breast and said, 'God, have mercy on me, a sinner.' "I tell you that this man, rather than the other, went home justified before God. For everyone who exalts himself will be humbled, and he who humbles himself will be exalted." (Luke 18:9-14 NIV emphasis, & unitalicized parenthetical definition added)*

Even if you engage in this exercise from a supposedly 'humble' standpoint, as I did, thinking *"I'm not <u>as bad</u> as him or her,"* you're still looking down on someone and exalting yourself. Jesus responded to the Pharisees who were questioning him for hanging out with sinners, *"Those who are well have no need of a physician, but those who are sick…For I did not come to call the righteous, but sinners, to repentance."* *(Matthew 9:12-13 NKJV)* Jesus was not conceding that they were in fact righteous, but the fact that they perceived themselves as such, rendered them beyond healing. "Those who suppose their souls to be without disease will not welcome the spiritual Physician."[5]

This is God's indictment on humanity:

"As it is written: 'None is righteous, no, not one; no one understands; no one seeks for God. All have turned aside; together they have become worthless; no one does good, not even one.' 'Their throat is an open grave; they use their tongues to deceive.' 'The venom of asps is under their lips.' 'Their mouth is full of curses and bitterness.' 'Their feet are swift to shed blood; in their paths are ruin and misery, and the way of peace they have not known.' 'There is no fear of God before their eyes.'" *(Romans 3:10-18 ESV)*

From my understanding, people had primarily one of two responses to the absolute holy character of Christ. Pretending to righteousness, the Pharisees were offended by the righteousness of God in the Person of Jesus. He called them to repentance by pointing out their inconsistencies. Jesus called them hypocrites or posers (cf. Matthew 23:13). But most, rather than repenting of their self-righteousness, clung tightly to their religious façade.

The other response was that of the common man, the "sinner." Jesus' character didn't reveal anything to them that they didn't already know. They knew that they failed to live up to God's standard. The very presence of Christ called them to repentance. Jesus' presence was healing for these. They were transformed and exhibited the fruit of repentance (e.g. Luke 19:8).

You just have to love the apostle Peter. He was so genuine, so blunt! I especially love His response to Jesus. After an earlier encounter with Christ, the character of Jesus must have been eating at him, when Peter later witnessed a miracle by Jesus (see Luke 5:5-7), he responded *"Go away from me, Lord; I am a sinful man!" (Luke 5:8 NIV)* It's almost as if Peter said, "Get away from me Lord, I'm gonna break your heart!" The Lord knew this and chose Peter anyway, or perhaps because of it.

According to all four Gospels, Peter did fail the Lord. Continuing with the Luke theme, after Jesus' arrest, Peter followed at a distance, and on three occasions, he was accused of having been a disciple of Jesus. On all three occasions Peter vehemently denied it. Luke records all three denials, but we'll focus on the last. *"But Peter said, 'Man, I don't know what you are talking about!' Immediately, while he was still speaking, a rooster crowed. The Lord turned, and looked at Peter. Then Peter remembered the Lord's word, how he said to him, 'Before the rooster crows you will deny me three times.' He went out, and wept bitterly." (Luke 22:60-62 WEB)*

When we measure ourselves by a right standard, we see how far off we truly are. *"...for all have sinned and fall short of the glory of God." (Romans 3:23 WEB)* Where can we look to find the glory of God from which we fall short? Hebrews 1:3 says *"The Son is the radiance of God's glory and the exact representation of his being." (NIV)* So in Jesus we find the glory of God. But we can't really start here, because most of us have a distorted view of Jesus that is based more upon who we are than Who He is. That is, we tend to imagine a Jesus that is like us. So we need to turn to something else. We catch a lesser, but more concrete glimpse of God's glory in the Ten Commandments. The Ten Commandments were given to Israel by God through Moses on Mount Sinai (Exodus chapter 20). But according to the following parenthetical statement found in Romans 2:13-15, the work of the law is written upon the hearts of mankind, albeit faintly. *"(for not the hearers of the law are just in the sight of God, but the doers of the law will be justified; for when Gentiles* (i.e. non-Jews), *who do not have the law, by nature do the things in the law, these, although not having the law, are a law to themselves, who show* **the work of the law written in their hearts**, *their conscience also bearing witness, and between themselves their thoughts accusing or else excusing them.)" (Romans 2:13-15 NKJV* **emphasis** *and clarification* **added**)

So the written law reinforces and reminds us of something we already have knowledge of, that is, our conscience. Let's look into the mirror of God's moral law and see how we measure up to His standard of goodness.

The Ten Commandments can be found in Exodus 20:3-17 and Deuteronomy 5:7-21. But for brevity sake I will use a condensed version, explaining the meaning of each, unless it's self-explanatory.

I. You shall have no other gods   Basically this cuts straight to worship. What we ascribe more glory to with our thoughts, attitudes and actions than God, and whatever consumes our thoughts is a god.

II. You shall not make for yourself an idol   This commandment is not warning us against having people whom we call idols, who we hold in high esteem, admire and imitate; though it might speak to situations where this behavior is taken to extremes. This commandment on its face is similar to the first, but it takes us to another level regarding the very nature of God. Nowadays we tend to make an idol with false ideas about Who God is. God is holy and as I touched on above, man has a tendency to create a god in his own image. For example, we tend to accentuate the love of God at the expense of other definitive characteristics associated with His holiness, and therefore we can't understand how God could allow souls to suffer in an eternal hell. Some false perceptions about God are formed by negative experiences with our own earthly father, or with a church. This leads to the other extreme that portrays God as a hate-filled tyrant who delights in the suffering of mankind and afterwards sends them to hell.

III. You shall not misuse the name of the LORD your God

Also known as blasphemy, on its face this refers to using the name of God flippantly or as a curse. (This was a serious offense that called for the death of the blasphemer, see Leviticus 24:11-16) But taken to another level this commandment speaks to how we live our lives. When we profess to be believers in Christ, but our lifestyle does not match this profession, we misuse the name of the Lord. (cf. Ezekiel 20:27)

IV. Observe the Sabbath day by keeping it holy It is my understanding that the law of the seventh-day Sabbath was unique to Israel's covenant with God and is not applicable for gentile believers. *"Therefore let no one pass judgment on you in questions of food and drink, or with regard to a festival or a new moon or a Sabbath. These are a shadow of the things to come, but the substance belongs to Christ." (Colossians 2:16-17 ESV)* For Christians, our Sabbath rest is not found in a day, but rather in the Person of Jesus Christ.

V. Honor your father and your mother

VI. You shall not murder This commandment is taken to another level by Jesus in Matthew 5:21-22. The apostle John elaborates in 1 John 3:15, *"Whoever hates his brother is a murderer, and you know that no murderer has eternal life remaining in him."* (WEB)

VII. You shall not commit adultery Jesus takes this to another level as well; *"You have heard that it was said to those of old, 'You shall not commit adultery.' But I say to you that whoever looks at a woman to lust for her has already committed adultery with her in his heart." (Matthew 5:27-28 NKJV)*

VIII. You shall not steal

IX. You shall not give false testimony against your neighbor Even though on its face, it seems that this command refers to courtroom testimony, its application goes beyond the courtroom. The need for honesty in all of our dealings is the natural implication of this commandment, as clearly expressed by other scripture passages. *"You shall not... deal falsely, or lie to one to another." (Leviticus 19:11 NIV)* This law is also reiterated in the New Testament. *"Therefore, having put away falsehood, let each one of you speak the truth with his neighbor, for we are members one of another." (Ephesians 4:25 ESV) "Do not lie to each other..." (Colossians 3:9 WEB)*

X. You shall not covet Covetousness is not simply desire; to covet means to desire wrongfully, inordinately, or without due regard for the rights of others. Covetousness comes from a discontented spirit.

With its eyes on another person's possessions, it is consumed with envy.

Mankind tends to imagine that God weighs our deeds on a type of scale, good versus bad, and that the balance of the scales determines our eternal destiny. But this very concept is an affront to the holy nature of God, Who cannot tolerate sin in His presence. It also undermines the seriousness of sin. Here are the kickers; *"If you really fulfill the royal law according to the Scripture, 'You shall love your neighbor as yourself,' you do well; but if you show partiality, you commit sin, and are convicted by the law as transgressors.* **For whoever shall keep the whole law, and yet stumble in one point, he is guilty of all.** *For He who said, "Do not commit adultery," also said, "Do not murder." Now if you do not commit adultery, but you do murder, you have become a transgressor of the law." (James 2:8-11 NKJV* **emphasis added***)* and *"For all who rely on works of the law are under a curse; for it is written,* **'Cursed be everyone who does not abide by all things written in the Book of the Law, and do them.'"** *(Galatians 3:10 ESV* **emphasis added***)*

Allow me to pull back the curtain on my own life and measure myself against the law, according to who I was before Christ changed my life. Working backwards, I was a covetous, lying thief, a fornicator, an adulterer at heart, a murderer at heart, a dishonoring, blasphemous, idolater. There is nothing honorable here. I had broken every commandment and yet as we saw above *"…whoever keeps the whole law and yet stumbles at just one point is guilty of breaking all of it." (James 2:10 NIV)*

When asked by a Pharisee which was the greatest commandment of the law, Jesus responded, *"'You shall love the Lord your God with all your heart, with all your soul, and with all your mind.' This is the first and great commandment. A second likewise is this, 'You shall love your neighbor as*

yourself.' The whole law and the prophets depend on these two commandments."
(Matthew 22:37-40 WEB)

Jesus reiterated two commands found in the Torah (i.e. the first 5 books of the Bible, written by Moses). The first and greatest commandment, found in Deuteronomy 6:4, encapsulates the first four of the Ten Commandments, while the second commandment, found in Deuteronomy 19:18, captures the intent behind the remaining six. The second is like the first because we love God by loving others, who are created in His image. As the apostle John puts it, *"If a man says, "I love God," and hates his brother, he is a liar; for he who doesn't love his brother whom he has seen, how can he love God whom he has not seen? This commandment we have from him, that he who loves God should also love his brother."* (1 John 4:20-21 WEB) Moreover, in establishing His law, using Himself as the example of ultimate love, Jesus takes this love to another level; *"A new commandment I give to you, that you love one another. Just as I have loved you, you also love one another. By this everyone will know that you are my disciples, if you have love for one another."* (John 13:34-35 WEB) Jesus' kind of love was a sacrificial kind, one that put the needs of others before His own. *Greater love has no one than this, that someone lay down his life for his friends. (John 15:13 ESV)*

Jesus' teachings are all about the next level. He, and the apostles, under His authority, took the law from 'you shall not,' to 'you ought.' This is made evident in the parable of the Good Samaritan, found in Luke 10:29-37. Based solely on the Mosaic Law, the priest and the Levite, who passed by on the other side of the road, did not sin against the man beaten half to death. They didn't do anything to the man, or for him. In fact, they ignored their moral duty and passed on the other side because, in keeping with Law of Moses, they didn't want to become ceremonially unclean. Whereas the

Samaritan, who had no such concerns, helped the man, thereby acting as a person ought. Jesus stated plainly what would become known as the golden rule. *"Do to others as you would have them do to you."* *(Luke 6:31 NIV)* So then, we have the sins of commission (you shall not), and the sins of omission (you ought to). *So whoever knows the right thing to do and fails to do it, for him it is sin. (James 4:17 ESV)* As we can see, our sin nature is the great equalizer. This nature is universal, affecting all of humanity.

Even so, I do not mean to imply that all sins are equal. There are degrees of sinfulness, measured along the moral standard. I wouldn't for a moment say that everyone is just as evil as everybody else. Rather, what I intend to convey is that we are all lawbreakers, and as such we are separated from God. We are His natural born enemies. *"But your iniquities have separated you and your God, and your sins have hidden his face from you, so that he will not hear." (Isaiah 59:2 WEB)*

I refer the Christian objector of my use of the law to **Appendix A.**

Real Tragedy

THE MORAL LAW tends to make us uneasy, as it highlights not only our shortcomings, but our sin nature. Our tendency is to excuse ourselves from the moral law. We say *"nobody's perfect."* But this very statement recognizes an innate understanding of a perfect standard. In measurements or mathematics, for example, we have a perfect standard in which all else, in these fields, finds its basis. This knowledge of the imperfection of the human condition is universal, even apart from the law. That's why I say it's innate. We know that something is not right with us, we are imperfect. This assumes that we have knowledge of perfection. As C.S. Lewis put it, "A man does not call a line crooked unless he has some idea of a straight line."[6] I contend that this is God-given and it is evidence of the fallen nature of mankind.

Then why do we turn away from the law, when it confirms what is already known innately? Perhaps because it confronts us head on, and we can no longer ignore the innate knowledge of a perfect standard. It forces us to recognize our own fallen nature.

Now since the introduction, where I told you that this wasn't about me, I have been trying to engage you through this writing, encouraging you to step out on a journey of faith. Occasionally, when I tell someone about the crash, their reply is, "that's tragic." The very title of this book, *From Tragedy to Triumph,* is not about me.

This is not just my story. Though yours will be different, if you so choose, this is your story too! In this world, we all experience tragedy. But the most tragic thing that occurred in history was the fall of mankind. That is the real tragedy from which all others stem! And what's even more tragic is the fact that we deny, minimize and rationalize our sin nature. We become complacent. The purpose of **The Bad News in the Mirror** section was to jar you out of this complacency, to wake you up to the fact that we are all condemned as guilty under the law, whether the law of stone or of conscience. We cannot experience the triumph if we don't acknowledge the reality of the tragedy.

To their peril, some deny the reality of the fall. They maintain that the world is progressing, that mankind is getting better. But a quick look at the state of society with its host of evils ought to bear out the fallacy of this position. Interestingly, the same people who declare that society is progressing towards utopia, are quick to argue for the removal of the Ten Commandments from all areas of public life, as if removal of the law written in stone will somehow remove the law inscribed upon our hearts. Also, those who would deny the existence of moral absolutes are quick to apply such absolutes to others when they are wronged. We are born with a conscience. Derived from Latin, *con* means with, and *science* means knowledge. Therefore, we are born *with knowledge* of right and wrong. It is innate. Based on the knowledge of a perfect standard, as I stated earlier.

However, I do not intend to imply that our parents and society at large don't help to develop or destroy our morals, as well as our conscience. They obviously do. But what we call the conscience obviously comes from a Source outside of nature. For example, one may be taught to discern right from wrong from a parent, but this standard didn't originate with the parent. It originated from another

Source. Similarly, just as a parent or teacher may teach mathematics, yet obviously math did not originate with them but from something already established, something very real.

According to the Judeo-Christian religions (Christianity, based on the revelation of the Jewish Messiah, Jesus, was born out of Judaism.), after God created the world and mankind, *"God saw everything that he had made, and, behold, it was very good." (Genesis 1:31 WEB)* We were created in the image of God and we were *"very good."* I contend that this is where we receive our intrinsic knowledge of the perfect standard. We were created to live in a perfect environment, in perfect fellowship with God. But something went terribly wrong.

According to Scripture, God warned Adam; *"You may surely eat of every tree of the garden, but of the tree of the knowledge of good and evil you shall not eat, for in the day that you eat of it you shall surely die." (Genesis 2:16-17 ESV)* Enter Satan, the fallen angel of whom we will talk about in the **Knowing Our Enemy** section. The account is recorded in Genesis chapter 3, but I'm going to summarize it for you. In the form of a serpent, Satan approached Eve in the Garden of Eden. He caused her to doubt God's word. He deceived Eve into believing God was holding out on them, that they could become gods if they ate of the forbidden fruit. Eve believed the lie and fell, by choosing to eat the fruit, directly disobeying the explicit commandment of God. Now a careful reading of Scripture reveals that Adam, as the spiritual head (cf. 1 Corinthians 11:3), may have had the opportunity to nullify the oath Eve had taken in eating of the fruit. *"If indeed she takes a husband, while bound by her vows or by a rash utterance from her lips by which she bound herself, and her husband hears it, and makes no response to her on the day that he hears, then her vows shall stand, and her agreements by which she bound herself shall stand. But if her husband overrules her on the day that he*

45

hears it, he shall make void her vow which she took and what she uttered with her lips, by which she bound herself, and the LORD will release her." (Numbers 30:6-8 NKJV) But Adam chose to abandon his position as spiritual head and follow after Eve.

Contrary to popular thought, Scripture reveals that Adam and Eve were together throughout the temptation and subsequent fall. *"When the woman saw that the fruit of the tree was good for food and pleasing to the eye, and also desirable for gaining wisdom, she took some and ate it. She also gave some to her husband,* **who was with her***, and he ate it." (Genesis 3:6 NIV* **emphasis added***)*

Returning to Genesis 2:17 quoted above, it's obvious from Scripture that God was referring to more than mere physical death when Adam sinned. We see that death had a dual meaning, because something else took place first – a spiritual death. They lost their perfect fellowship with God, as well as their status as perfect creatures. Adam traded freedom for slavery. He committed high treason against heaven! Adam traded God not for self, as the devil deceived Eve into believing, but rather he traded God for Satan. When we were born into this world, we inherited this spiritual death through our first father Adam. We inherited this sin of treason against God. Therefore, we are born spiritually dead.

Creation also bears the curse of the fall of man. God arranged it so that when mankind fell, creation fell with us. This was to serve as a reminder that we were not created for this fallen world. Creation groans with natural disasters; earthquakes, tornadoes, floods, hurricanes and the like, just as we groan under the consequences of sin.

"The creation waits in eager expectation for the sons of God to be revealed. For the creation was subjected to frustration, not by its own choice, but by the will of

the one who subjected it, in hope that the creation itself will be liberated from its bondage to decay and brought into the glorious freedom of the children of God. We know that **the whole creation has been groaning** *as in the pains of childbirth right up to the present time. Not only so, but we ourselves, who have the firstfruits of the Spirit, groan inwardly as we wait eagerly for our adoption as sons, the redemption of our bodies." (Romans 8:19-23 NIV* **emphasis added**)

According to Christ, tragedies are meant to confront us with the reality of our mortality, and urge us towards repentance. *"Now there were some present at the same time who told him about the Galileans, whose blood Pilate had mixed with their sacrifices. Jesus answered them, 'Do you think that these Galileans were worse sinners than all the other Galileans, because they suffered such things? I tell you, no, but unless you repent, you will all perish in the same way. Or those eighteen, on whom the tower in Siloam fell, and killed them; do you think that they were worse offenders than all the men who dwell in Jerusalem? I tell you, no,* **but, unless you repent, you will all perish in the same way.'"** *(Luke 13:1-5 WEB* **emphasis added**)

One purpose of the moral law is to guide and protect us as we sojourn through this fallen world. However, its primary purpose is to highlight our sinfulness. It draws attention to the fact that we are a mess and that we are unable to clean ourselves up. The purpose of the law was not to provide a way for mankind to obtain salvation, but to point out our need for a savior. *"Therefore no one will be declared righteous in his sight by observing the law; rather, through the law we become conscious of sin." (Romans 3:20 NIV)* Some feel as if they need to clean themselves up before coming to God, but it is impossible to make ourselves righteous before a holy God. Indeed, *"But we are all like an unclean thing, and all our righteousnesses are like filthy rags..." (Isaiah 64:6*

NKJV) God invites us to come to as we are and He will clean us up. He has provided us with the Way of triumph!

In Adam, we are born slaves to our sinful nature. In John 8:34 Jesus said, *"Most assuredly, I say to you, whoever commits sin is a slave of sin." (NKJV)* "No man knows how bad he is till he has tried very hard to be good. Only those who try to resist temptation know how strong it is."[7] It's not directly revealed in Scripture, but it is obvious that behind the satanic plot that led to the fall of man was more than just mankind. Although, we can be sure that the image of God reflected in man enraged Satan, his ultimate aim was God Himself. It appears that behind it was Satan's attempt to divide the heart of God. God is holy; His holiness constitutes all of His attributes, including His unity. This demands that all of the attributes of God be in perfect balance. The basic attributes that Satan intended to divide were His perfect justice and His perfect love. Satan seemingly wanted to create a conflict in the heart of God by turning God's objects of love against Him, causing an imbalance in His holy nature.

I pray that this and the previous section were adequate to convince you of the depravity of mankind and that we all share a depraved nature. This nature is innate; that is, it is something we are born with. I've asked you take an honest look within yourself to confirm this reality. Better yet, allow God to search you, for in Jeremiah chapter 17:9, the Lord spoke through the prophet, revealing; *"The heart is deceitful above all things, and desperately wicked; Who can know it? I, the LORD, search the heart, I test the mind, even to give every man according to his ways, according to the fruit of his doings." (NKJV)* The psalmist understood this, that's why he wrote and prayed, *"Search me, O God, and know my heart; Try me, and know my anxieties; and see if there is any wicked way in me, and lead me in the way everlasting." (Psalm 139:23-24 NKJV)*

A Time of Darkness

Why, O LORD, do you stand far away?
Why do you hide yourself in times of trouble? (Psalm 10:1 ESV)

"To You I will cry, O Lord my Rock: Do not be silent to me, Lest, if You are
silent to me, I become like those who go down to the pit." (Psalm 28:1 NIV)

I DON'T ENCOURAGE you to jump ahead, but chronologically, this section should have come after the **War.** However, I want to bring you along with me on my journey of understanding and to do that, it seemed appropriate to insert this section here. In the previous two sections, I have tried to simulate the spiritual reality which I was confronted with after this **Time of Darkness.** But even now, you may not be adequately prepared for all that's written in this section. Nevertheless, it is my hope and prayer, that by the end of the sections following this, you will have a better understanding.

Not long after the spiritual warfare described in the section entitled **War**, I was thrown into a state of further despair as I could no longer feel God's presence. God had gone 'silent' on me. It seemed as if my prayers were just hitting the ceiling. This was almost as fearful as my previous state.

I was aware that the Christian faith is based on more than mere feelings and that God promised *"I will in no way leave you, neither will I in any way forsake you." (Hebrews 13:5 WEB)* Still, the God-forsaken feeling ruled the moment. The emotions of loneliness and despair were so overwhelming that doubt of my salvation crept in, which also gave way to fear. I was so in the moment, it was like I forgot that God had always been faithful, even when I was faithless. I began to question things; did I do something to lose God's favor? Was I ever truly saved? What did I have to do to earn back God's favor?

I'm not sure how long this lasted, but long enough that I sought out the advice of a friend of mine, Tom, who pastored Immanuel, in Roseville. I didn't share all of my doubts and questions with Pastor Tom. I only shared that God seemed distant and I was struggling with depression as a result. He reassured me that such times of darkness were not unusual, and advised me to read the Psalms, that King David struggled under such times.

I did so, and the Psalms brought me some comfort, but I still couldn't shake the feeling of abandonment. Then one day, I was sitting silently in the living room, while my parents were in the dining room. Suddenly, tears just started streaming down my face. I didn't see or hear anything, but it was as if God revealed His holiness to me and I was caught up in the fear of the Lord (cf. 2 Corinthians 5:11). Perhaps it wasn't a revelation, but more of a realization. I just kept repeating, "I can't do it, I can't do it."

In this state of realization, I was completely overwhelmed. I could identify with the prophet Isaiah during his vision of the Lord, when he cried, *"Woe to me!"* ... *"I am ruined! For I am a man of unclean lips, and I live among a people of unclean lips, and my eyes have seen the King, the LORD Almighty." (Isaiah 6:5 NIV)* When one realizes the complete righteousness and holiness of the Lord, he ought to immediately see himself in comparison and be utterly ruined.

I was confronted with the full *gravity* of my sinfulness. I was brought low, humbled before the Lord. This humility gave way to a true understanding of the Gospel and the concepts of grace and mercy. I realized that apart from the mercy of God, in Christ, the wrath of God would rest upon me, *"What a wretched man I am! Who will deliver me out of the body of this death? I thank God through Jesus Christ, our Lord!" (Romans 7:24-25a WEB)*

I realized that even though I accepted Christ as my Savior, I was still trying to earn God's grace. When one grasps the meaning of grace, which is unmerited favor, he begins to understand how contradictory and senseless the idea of earning grace truly is. In this place of utter ruin, where I was, I realized that a more accurate definition of grace is "favor against merit." For me, grace moved beyond a mere concept to a wonderful reality to experience.

"...what can a man give in return for his soul?" (Matthew 16:26 ESV) "Who has ever given to God, that God should repay him?" (Romans 11:34, Job 41:11 NIV) "For by grace you have been saved through faith. And this is not your own doing; it is the gift of God, **not a result of works, so that no one may boast.***" (Ephesians 2:8-9 ESV* **emphasis added***)*

I know that this will be a point of contention for those who are beholden to certain religious ideologies. But the implication of these verses and many others like them is that the redemptive work is finished! There is nothing we need to do or can do, to add to it! *"It is finished." (John 19:30 WEB)* Indeed, if we were able to add to grace, it would completely nullify grace. *"But if it is by grace, it is no longer on the basis of works; otherwise grace would no longer be grace." (Romans 11:6 ESV)* This section doesn't seem like an appropriate place to expound on or defend the truth of the finished work and sufficiency of Christ, but I will definitely return to it.

Truly, the Gospel is an assault on pride. It was difficult and humbling to realize that I do not have any control over my salvation, that I cannot earn anything from God. I came to the understanding of the complete sufficiency of the crucifixion, resurrection and ascension of Jesus Christ. According to Hebrews 12:2, Jesus is *"the author and finisher of our faith," (NKJV)* and in regards to salvation, religion is useless, because it operates from the premise of man working his way to God – man achieving, attaining or meriting salvation. Whereas in Christianity God came to be mankind's salvation, as the Savior. Thus, authentic Christianity is not a religion, but rather a relationship with God based upon faith in Jesus Christ.

I have given you a preview of the Gospel; I will elaborate more on it in the following sections.

The Beginning of Romance

"So we have come to know and to believe the love that God has for us. God is love." (1 John 4:16 ESV)

"God is the most loving person in the universe. That means he's also the most sensitive person in the universe. Love is making yourself vulnerable. The more you love, the more you can get hurt." (No Compromise: The Keith Green Story; Melody Green and David Hazard)[8]

IT IS MY prayer that the next few sections don't obscure the simple beauty of the Gospel (cf. 2 Corinthians 11:3). There is a danger of this when we multiply words in an effort to explain the Gospel. Nevertheless, there is much beauty to be pressed into when our souls seek understanding. Though it is not necessary for salvation that we understand the full glory of the Gospel, or that such understanding is even humanly possible, such an endeavor is most profitable. My purpose here is to reveal but only a glimpse of the glory of the Gospel, not its fullness. The thought of trying to press into full glory of the Gospel is mind blowing and beyond my purpose or ability in writing.

I do not have all the answers. I don't pretend for a second to understand everything, or much of anything for that matter. A lot of what happens in this world is beyond human comprehension. God declared that this would be the case, *"For my thoughts are not your thoughts, neither are your ways my ways,' declares the LORD. 'As the heavens are higher than the earth, so are my ways higher than your ways and my thoughts than your thoughts.'" (Isaiah 55:8-9 NIV)* But regarding the Word of God, reading under the illuminated guidance of the Holy Spirit, I have some understanding of it. Nevertheless, I want you to keep in mind that I am liable to err. You don't have to agree with everything I have written. If my writing should depart from that of the Holy Bible, let the Bible take precedence. I am still growing in my understanding of Scripture.

That being said, I should note that I interpret Scripture in a plain, normative, grammatical, historical sense. Words have a clear meaning, which means they must have an objective, unbiased way to be interpreted. Otherwise, all written communication would be meaningless and illogical. The Bible, being a collection of 66 books, contains different literary styles. It is filled with metaphors or word pictures, as one would expect in a case where an eternal infinite God is stooping down in an effort to reveal Himself to finite fallen mankind. When metaphors are employed, their meaning is usually pretty easy to understand. For example, *"I say to God my **Rock.**" (Psalm 42:9 NKJV **emphasis added**)* The psalmist isn't saying God is a rock, rather he is saying that God is like a rock – his foundation, sure and strong. Jesus often used parables to teach eternal truth. To interpret such passages literally would be foolish, and would completely ignore the grammatical structure of the Bible.

Nevertheless, there are those who disagree with the normal/plain-sense meaning. These people often seek to spiritualize the Bible by allegorizing, or reading symbolism into Scripture when the text doesn't necessitate such an interpretation. This method allows them to pick and choose what they believe. This form of interpretation essentially renders the Bible meaningless, by making the reader god. A normal/plain-sense interpretation in no way negates the fact that the Bible contains passages that are allegorical, symbolic, or poetic in nature, but the context of these passages make it clear when such literary devices are being used (e.g. Galatians 4:21-31; Song of Songs). A rule of interpretation that I subscribe to is "if the plain meaning makes sense, seek no other sense, lest you end up with nonsense." Neither does a plain reading of the Bible negate the fact that different passages will take on different significance and meaning to different individuals during different times in life. This attests to the personal nature of God, as well as to the living nature of His word. *"For the word of God is living and active, and sharper than any two-edged sword, piercing even to the dividing of soul and spirit, of both joints and marrow, and is able to discern the thoughts and intentions of the heart."* (Hebrews 4:12 WEB)

"All Scripture is God-breathed and is useful for teaching, rebuking, correcting and training in righteousness, so that the man of God may be thoroughly equipped for every good work." (2 Timothy 3:16-17 NIV) Another factor that's important to acknowledge while interpreting Scripture, is that while all Scripture is for me, not all Scripture is about me. *"For whatever things were written before were written for our learning, that we through the patience and comfort of the Scriptures might have hope." (Romans 15:4 NKJV)* *"Now these things happened to them as an example, but they were written down for our instruction, on whom the end of the ages has come." (1 Corinthians 10:11 ESV)*

Now bear with me as I seek to reveal a glimpse of the beauty of the Gospel, the Real Triumph! Let's start at **The Beginning of Romance.**

God is the original Romantic. I contend that all pure human ideals of romance come from Him, and fall wildly short of His nature. We often pervert what real romance is. We have a tendency to replace romance with lust and sex.

Appealing to the question of why God created free beings, I turn to this eloquent quote from C.S. Lewis; "God created things which had free will. That means creatures which can go wrong or right. Some people think they can imagine a creature which was free but had no possibility of going wrong, but I can't. If a thing is free to be good it's also free to be bad. And free will is what has made evil possible. Why, then, did God give them free will? Because free will, though it makes evil possible, is also the only thing that makes possible any love or goodness or joy worth having. A world of automata – of creatures that worked like machines – would hardly be worth creating. The happiness which God designs for His higher creatures is the happiness of being freely, voluntarily united to Him and to each other in an ecstasy of love and delight compared with which the most rapturous love between a man and a woman on this earth is mere milk and water. And for that they've got to be free."[9]

We were made by God for God, created to be in a love relationship with Him, enjoying Him forever. But love that is forced upon another is not love at all. God created us with free will, giving us a choice. We chose wrongly. Have you ever had a romantic love for another person, which you showed in word and deed, only for that person to reject you? That heartache you felt is only a glimpse of the ache God feels when you reject Him, and He feels it continually. God loves you. He aches with desire to establish a relationship with you and He never gets over you. Yet, He honored and continues to honor our choice when we reject Him because that is the essence of love. Come with me as we see how Scripture describes our original rejection of God, and His response.

Let's start with Genesis 3:7, which describes the immediate impact of the Fall; *"Their eyes were opened, and they both knew that they were naked. They sewed fig leaves together, and made coverings for themselves."* *(WEB)* As soon as Adam and Eve ate the forbidden fruit, they immediately lost all fellowship with God. They experienced spiritual death. Spiritual death is the separation of the soul and spirit from God. The fig leaves that they sewed together can be likened to religion – mankind's feeble attempts to repair fellowship with the Holy God.

Next, we see the first glimpse of the romantic heart of God kick into effect. He didn't abandon mankind, but pursued him. *"And they heard the sound of the LORD God walking in the garden in the cool of the day, and Adam and his wife hid themselves from the presence of the LORD God among the trees of the garden. Then the LORD God called to Adam and said to him, 'Where are you?'"* *(Genesis 3:8-9 NKJV)* God is all-knowing. He knew where Adam was and what he had done. These questions were meant to confront mankind with the gravity of the choice he had made. The question remains, *"Where are you?"*

"He answered, 'I heard you in the garden, and I was afraid because I was naked; so I hid.' And he said, 'Who told you that you were naked? Have you eaten from the tree that I commanded you not to eat from?'" *(Genesis 3:10-11 NIV)* If we look back at Genesis 3:5, we see that the serpent promised Eve that they would have knowledge of good and evil, and so the conscience was birthed. God wanted mankind to know that this knowledge was a direct consequence of breaking His commandment. He afflicted man's new-found conscience so that he realized he had traded perfect fellowship with God, for fear and guilt.

Before the fall, Adam ruled the world as God's representative. But when Adam sinned, he abdicated his authority and subjugated this realm to Satan's authority. Since the fall, Satan's influence has dominated society. *"...the whole world lies under the sway of the wicked one."* *(1 John 5:19 NKJV)*. Scripture calls the devil *"the ruler of this world"* *(John 12:31 & 14:30 NKJV)*, *"The god of this age"* *(2 Corinthians 4:4 NIV)*, and *"...the ruler of the kingdom of the air, the spirit who is now at work in those who are disobedient."* *(Ephesians 2:2 NIV)*. This is not to say that he is sovereign over the world. Only God is. It means that God, in His infinite wisdom, has sovereignly allowed Satan to operate in this world with an agenda, within the boundaries He has set for him. Understanding this truth helps explain why the world is in such chaos.

C.S. Lewis understood this world as; "Enemy-occupied territory – that is what this world is. Christianity is the story of how the rightful king has landed; you might say landed in disguise, and is calling us all to take part in a great campaign of sabotage. When you go to church you are really listening-in to secret wireless from our friends: that is why the enemy is so anxious to prevent us from going."[10]

So, as the Lord began to pronounce the consequences (or curse) that resulted from the fall of man, he began with the serpent. The second half of this curse is most revealing; *"And I will put enmity between you and the woman, and between your seed and her Seed; He shall bruise your head, and you shall bruise His heel."* *(Genesis 3:15 NKJV)* This is God's declaration of war! In this passage, He lets Satan, as well as us, know that He's gonna fight for the love of mankind.

Let's dissect this declaration. Notice how in this passage the focus shifts from the Seed, which can be read as offspring, to focus on singular Person; *"He"* and *"His."* This verse is a foreshadowing of the Gospel, as well as the first biblical reference to a messianic figure, a Savior. This Messiah would bruise (literally crush) the head of the serpent. The bruised heel is a reference to the crucifixion and death of Christ. It's likened to a bruise because it wouldn't be permanent, whereas the bruise to the head of the serpent crushed under the heal of Messiah would be fatal. An inference to the virgin birth of the Messiah is also found in the fact that God refers to the Seed of the woman. Women don't have seed or semen. This would be a miraculous birth through the Holy Spirit.

Finally, it was retribution time. Adam and Eve should have died physically as well as spiritually. But in Genesis 3:21 we read that, *"The LORD God made garments of skin for Adam and his wife and clothed them." (NIV)* In this act, God laid the foundation for substitutionary sacrifices. In this passage, we see the pattern for all salvation history. God took a sacrificial animal. He slew it before the eyes of Adam and Eve and wrapped the skins about their naked bodies. No doubt, at that time, God gave them instructions about sacrifice as a covering of sins. The first century Jewish reader would have seen an obvious parallel with the Levitical sacrificial system. *"For the life of the flesh is in the blood; and I have given it to you on the altar to make atonement for your souls: for it is the blood that makes atonement by reason of the life." (Leviticus 17:11 WEB)* It's important to recognize that God took the initiative in offering atonement (i.e. reconciliation) for the sins of Adam and Eve. This sacrifice only covered their sins. It wasn't adequate to remove them (cf. Hebrews 10:4). But in it God established the life exchange principle that we can only draw near to Him by blood, for *"without the shedding of blood there is no forgiveness of sins." (Hebrews 9:22 ESV)* This also imperfectly prefigured the Gospel, what I call the Real Triumph.

As we see, according to Scripture, even before God drove man out of the garden, He began His relentless pursuit of him to restore a broken relationship. While there are many other beautiful foreshadows of the Gospel in the Old Testament, I hope that this section was sufficient to show you God's heart for you. Finally, I pray you're prepared to press into the Real Triumph with greater appreciation and comprehension.

The Real Triumph

For God so loved the world, that he gave his only Son, that whoever believes in him should not perish but have eternal life. (John 3:16 ESV)

And having disarmed the powers and authorities, he made a public spectacle of them, triumphing over them by the cross." (Colossians 2:15 NIV emphasis added)

WE WERE BORN into a world at war; an unseen struggle is under way between good and evil for the souls of men and women! Contrary to popular thought, although we bear His image, we are not born as children of God. It is my understanding that at birth we are essentially spiritual bastards. However, we are not spiritually neutral. We inherited Adam's fallen nature; *"Therefore as sin entered into the world through one man, and death through sin; and so death passed to all men, because all sinned. (Romans 5:12 WEB)* Mankind has a propensity towards sin, and, it seems, an inevitability to sin. Sin is an act of self-will against the conscience. Therefore, an infant is incapable of sin. So it follows that there must be an age of accountability. What is it? God knows, I do not. As soon as we sin, the devil claims us as his children. Leaving this for now, I elaborate more on the fallacy of all mankind being children of God in the section **Of Great Consequence.**

61

In the last section, **The Beginning of Romance,** we established that God is love and that He pursues us. What could God give us to show us that He is the perfect lover? He could give us nothing less than Himself! *"He saw that there was no man, and wondered that there was no intercessor; therefore His own arm brought salvation for Him; and His own righteousness, it sustained Him." (Isaiah 59:16 NKJV)* God's perfect pursuit of us was revealed in the Person of Jesus Christ, the revelation of the very heart of God. The Bible is an epic love story!

According to Old Testament prophecy and New Testament Scripture, Jesus is Messiah, Savior and God. I will approach the next couple of sections with a keen focus on the Person of Jesus Christ – Who He is, what He accomplished for you, and how to apply it. I am assuming that you have some familiarity with Christianity. Therefore, I have not set out to rewrite or regurgitate the Gospels. If you are not familiar with Christianity, Jesus and/or the controversy surrounding Him, I encourage you to read through the Gospel according to John, as well as Paul's letter to the Romans.

It's a mind blowing beautiful reality to be grasped, to come to terms with the eternal God sending His very heart, His only Son, to live a perfect life here on earth. Jesus lived the life that we were unable to live, the life that God's holy nature demands. Jesus kept the law perfectly, redeeming us from the law by becoming a curse for us. *"Christ redeemed us from the curse of the law, having become a curse for us. For it is written, 'Cursed is everyone who hangs on a tree.'" (Galatians 3:13 WEB)* Moreover, by His perfect sacrifice, Jesus fulfilled the law in its entirety. *"Do not think that I have come to abolish the Law or the Prophets; I have not come to abolish them but to **fulfill them**. I tell you the truth, until heaven and earth disappear, not the smallest letter, not the least stroke of a pen, will by any means disappear from the Law **until everything is accomplished**." (Matthew 5:17-18 NIV **emphasis added**)*

Testifying to His sinlessness, Jesus challenged his enemies, *"Which of you convicts me of sin?"* *(John 8:46 WEB)* The men who were closest to Jesus also testified; *"...him who had no sin"* *(2 Corinthians 5:21 NIV)* *"He committed no sin, and no deceit was found in his mouth."* *(1 Peter 2:22 NIV)*, *"...in him there is no sin."* *(1 John 3:5 ESV)*, and, *"For we do not have a high priest who is unable to sympathize with our weaknesses, but one who in every respect has been tempted as we are, yet without sin."* *(Hebrews 4:13 ESV)*

Jesus Christ, the very heart of God, *"who is in the bosom of the Father"* *(John 1:18 NKJV)*, is God Himself Who took on flesh. *"Let this mind be in you which was also in Christ Jesus, who, being in the form of God, did not consider it robbery to be equal with God, but made Himself of no reputation, taking the form of a bondservant, and coming in the likeness of men."* *(Philippians 2:5-7 NKJV)* Jesus is the *Son of God (Matthew 4:3 WEB)* and the *Son of Man. (Matthew* 8:20 WEB) He is fully God and fully man. He is God incarnate, *"For in Him all the fullness of the Godhead dwells bodily..."* *(Colossians 2:9 WEB)* These are but a few of many scripture passages indicating that the Messiah is God, but there are also many prophetic scriptures in the Old Testament indicating that the Messiah would be God. I don't want to spend too much space on this, because I believe that if you read the Bible, and sincerely ask God, that the Holy Spirit will confirm this truth.

However, I will offer a few examples of Old Testament prophecy indicating that the Messiah would be God. Isaiah 7:14 says *"Therefore the Lord himself will give you a sign: The virgin will be with child and will give birth to a son, and will call him Immanuel."* *(NIV)* Immanuel literally means "God with us." Isaiah 9:6 states *"For to us a child is born. To us a son is given; and the government will be on his shoulders. His name will be called Wonderful Counselor, Mighty God, Everlasting Father, Prince of Peace."* *(WEB)* And Micah 5:2 reads *"But you, Bethlehem*

Ephrathah, though you are little among the thousands of Judah, yet out of you shall come forth to Me the One to be Ruler in Israel, Whose goings forth are from of old, from everlasting." (NKJV) "The One" referred to here would come from eternity. He'd be eternal. These Scriptures found their fulfillment in Jesus. See Matthew 1:23 and 2:6. He lived and walked among us in the first century.

This Jesus was crucified on a Roman cross. It was our sin that crucified Christ and broke the heart of God. Many like to ponder the physical aspect of the death of Christ. Horrific though it was, the worst part of Christ's death was not physical, but spiritual, as he took on the sin of the world. Mark 15:34 records *"And at the ninth hour Jesus cried with a loud voice, 'Eloi, Eloi, lama sabachthani?' which means, 'My God, my God, why have you forsaken me?"* (ESV)

In this moment, Christ experienced a type of spiritual death as He was separated from the Father. It was only a type of spiritual death because Jesus, being the second Person of the Triune Godhead, coequal with the Father and the Holy Spirit, had spiritual life in Himself. *"For as the Father has life in himself, so he has granted the Son also to have life in himself."* (John 5:26 ESV) Speaking of His physical life, Jesus said; *"Therefore the Father loves me, because I lay down my life, that I may take it again. No one takes it away from me, but I lay it down by myself. I have power to lay it down, and I have power to take it again. I received this commandment from my Father."* (John 10:17-18 WEB)

Nevertheless, like Adam, Jesus' relationship with the Father was severed. God the Father turned His back on His Son! For the first time ever, throughout eternity past, the Triune nature of the Godhead was disrupted on our behalf! Our finite minds are unable to understand the magnitude of this event! God was literally broken for us! With this act, God showed His hatred for sin along with His love for sinners. *"This is how God showed his love among us: He sent his one* and only Son into the world that we might live through him. This is love: not that we loved God, but that he loved us and sent his Son as an atoning sacrifice **(propitiation)** for our sins." (1 John 4:9-10 NIV **parenthetical reference mine, from NKJV)**

There are many different facets, dimensions or aspects we could focus on to gain insight into the depth of the triumph that happened on the cross almost two thousand years ago. But for the sake of brevity and simplicity, let's focus on three key concepts; reconciliation, propitiation and redemption.

God once again provided a sacrifice to atone (i.e. to make amends) for our sins, but not just any sacrifice. This was the Sacrifice to end all sacrifices. *"Unlike the other high priests, he does not need to offer sacrifices day after day, first for his own sins, and then for the sins of the people. He sacrificed for their sins once for all when he offered himself."* (Hebrews 7:27 NIV) Jesus died physically and in type, spiritually, for a time, so that we would have the opportunity to become fully alive. That is, so that God might impart to us spiritual life and reconcile us unto Himself.

Reconciliation is the act of making peace between two parties that were once in opposition. By throwing in with Satan when we sinned, we declared ourselves as God's enemies. Our sin so separated us from God that only God Himself could restore the relationship that we forfeited. *"All this is from God, **who through Christ reconciled us to himself** and gave us the ministry of reconciliation; that is, **in Christ God was reconciling the world to himself**, not counting their trespasses against them, and entrusting to us the message of reconciliation. Therefore, we are ambassadors for Christ, God making his appeal through us. **We implore you on behalf of Christ, be reconciled to God.** For our sake he made him to be sin who knew no sin,* so that in him we might become the righteousness of God." (2 Corinthians 5:18-21 ESV **emphasis added**) cf. Isaiah 59:16

As I touched on in **The Real Tragedy,** God told Adam "*...you must not eat from the tree of the knowledge of good and evil, for when you eat of it you will surely die." (Genesis 2:17 NIV)* We read in Romans 6:23 that "*the wages of sin is death." (WEB)* So God was owed a death, or more accurately, as I hope I have established, God was owed the life of a righteous man. As enemies of God, unable to pay the debt we owed, God's wrath rightly rested upon us. By the way, it's not necessary or even accurate to view God as saving us from Himself. Rather, a more accurate portrayal would be of God, a loving Father, rescuing His children from the consequences of sin, while keeping His holy nature intact.

Earlier I wrote how Satan attempted to create a conflict in the heart of God by dividing His perfect justice and His perfect love. At this point I'd like to introduce you to another theological term; propitiation. I have it highlighted in parentheses in the quote of 1 John 4:9-10 above, which is the proper word construction here, as found in the NKJV.

Propitiation is a term denoting a sacrifice, by which God is satisfied or appeased, by which He is able to pardon sinners. Propitiation renders God's character consistent, it doesn't procure His love or make Him loving. He is love. By sending Jesus as propitiation, God proved His holiness, making His perfect love consistent with His perfect justice. On the cross, we see the manifestation of God's wrath in union with His love.

Does this mean that God was somehow less than holy before the death of Christ? Absolutely not! This is why Scripture portrays Jesus as being "*the Lamb slain from the foundation of the world." (Revelation 13:8 NKJV)* The all-knowing God, in His foreknowledge, was perfectly prepared for Satan's rebellion and the fall of mankind and had predetermined to use it for His glory. Therefore, before any of it took place, He ensured that His holiness, His character, would remain intact under assault. The crucifixion was complete in eternity past, but God introduced it into history almost 2000 years ago so that we might be saved. *"But when the time had fully come, God sent his Son, born of a woman, born under law..." (Galatians 4:4 NIV)* "He indeed was foreordained before the foundation of the world, but was manifest in these last times for you..." (1 Peter 1:20 NKJV)* God demonstrated His righteousness and love on the cross. (cf. Romans 3:25 NKJV)

How were people saved before the crucifixion? As we have already seen, *"by the deeds of the law no flesh will be justified in His sight, for by the law is the knowledge of sin." (Romans 3:20 NKJV)* Therefore, it is my understanding that prior to the introduction of the crucifixion of Christ in history, the basis of salvation was still the blood of Christ. The requirement for salvation has always been faith.

However, before the crucifixion, the content of mankind's faith was limited to the promise of the coming Messiah, a Redeemer who would deal with the problem of sin. *"For what does the Scripture say? 'Abraham believed God, and it was accounted to him for righteousness.'" (Romans 4:3 NKJV cf. Genesis 15:6)* As I explained in **The Beginning of Romance,** God took the initiative in clothing Adam and Eve in garments of animal skin (cf. Genesis 3:21). By receiving the garments, Adam demonstrated his trust in and acceptance of God's solution for sin, thus restoring their relationship. As I pointed out earlier, this imperfectly prefigured the Gospel, specifically the crucifixion of Jesus the Messiah. Therefore, it is safe to say that Adam put his faith the Lord's promised Messiah, who is first revealed Genesis 3:15. Similarly, the Levitical sacrificial system (cf. Leviticus 17:11), while not sufficient for the removal of sin (cf.

67

Hebrews 10:4), pointed to the coming Messiah (cf. Hebrews 9:18-26). Those who put their faith in this temporary and imperfect system, put their faith in Christ.

According to the Bible, Jesus came to rescue us from sin, which necessitated the defeat of Satan, the author of sin. *"For this purpose the Son of God was manifested, that He might destroy the works of the devil." (1 John 3:8 NKJV)* To do this, God, like the ultimate judo player, used Satan's strength against him. *"Since the children have flesh and blood, he too shared in their humanity so that* **by his death he might destroy him who holds the power of death—that is, the devil**— *and free those who all their lives were held in slavery by their fear of death." (Hebrews 2:14-15 NIV* **emphasis added***)* By way of the cross, God turned evil against itself and brought about the perfect solution. He made atonement for sins, He conquered death, He triumphed over the devil, and He laid the foundation for hope! *"And having disarmed the powers and authorities, he made a public spectacle of them, triumphing over them by the cross." (Colossians 2:15 NIV)*

For those who are unaware, judo is a martial art that emphasizes the use of quick movement and leverage to throw an opponent. Its techniques are generally intended to turn an opponent's force to one's own advantage rather than to oppose it directly. I love the following quote by Henri Blocher, and you'll be able to see that I derived much inspiration for the previous paragraph from it.

"Evil is conquered as evil because God turns it back upon itself. He makes the supreme crime, the murder of the only righteous person, the very operation that abolishes sin. The maneuver is utterly unprecedented. No more complete victory could be imagined. God responds in the indirect way that is perfectly suited to the ambiguity of evil. He entraps the deceiver in his own wiles. Evil, like a judoist, takes advantage of the power of the good, which it perverts; the Lord, like a supreme champion, replies by using the very grip of the opponent."[11]

Interestingly, this move by God of using Satan's own weapon to defeat him was foreshadowed in David's victory over Goliath. *"So David prevailed over the Philistine with a sling and a stone, and struck the Philistine and killed him. But there was no sword in the hand of David. Therefore, David ran and stood over the Philistine, took his sword and drew it out of its sheath and killed him, and cut off his head with it." (1 Samuel 17:50-51 NKJV)*

If you're anything like me, you may be wondering why Satan would have Christ crucified if he was to be defeated by His death? You're assuming, like I used to, that Satan, being able to quote Scripture (cf. Matthew 4:6), has a perfect understanding of it. But God couched the crucifixion and resurrection of Christ in prophetic language (see Isaiah 53; Daniel 9:26) and since Satan approaches Scripture in unbelief, he understands very little of it. The same principle applies to mankind when he reads Scripture in unbelief, for *"The man without the Spirit does not accept the things that come from the Spirit of God, for they are foolishness to him, and he cannot understand them, because they are spiritually discerned." (1 Corinthians 2:14 NIV)* Ultimately, my argument regarding Satan is summed up in 1 Corinthians 2:8, *"None of the rulers of this age understood this, for if they had, they would not have crucified the Lord of glory." (ESV)* Satan is one such ruler who didn't understand how his prophesied defeat would be accomplished.

Let's now turn our attention to redemption. To redeem something means to recover it by payment or some other means of satisfaction. A simple definition would be *to buy back.* Redemption, like all other theological concepts, is foreshadowed in the Old Testament. Probably the most obvious foreshadowing is that of the Passover lamb, by which the Israelites were redeemed from the slavery they endured in Egypt (see Exodus 12). Likewise, we were slaves to sin and Christ is referred to as *"the Lamb of God." (John 1:29, 36 WEB)*

But I'd like to look at another often overlooked example of redemption, found in Hosea. In order to demonstrate His love for His chosen people, Israel, when God called the prophet Hosea, He told him to marry a prostitute (Hosea 1:2). From my understanding, God did not command Hosea to marry an immoral woman against his will. Rather, Hosea already had a desire to marry this particular woman. God just gave him the "go ahead," with a warning that she would be unfaithful.

Using Hosea's life, God portrayed Himself as a lover, a husband, whose wife had been unfaithful. Just as God loves His people, Hosea sincerely loved his wife, and her unfaithfulness broke his heart. She had sunk so low as to sell herself into slavery. She was now the property of another man, whom, in modern language, we would call a pimp. In Hosea 3:1, the Lord tells Hosea to seek out his adulterous wife and show his love towards her again. Hosea finds her in slavery and Hosea 3:2 reads, *"So I bought her for myself for fifteen pieces of silver and a homer and a half of barley." (WEB)* Hosea redeemed his unfaithful wife and reaffirmed his commitment to her.

Similarly, we have gone astray from God. We have sold ourselves as slaves to sin, we are like whores and sin is our brutal pimp. But God has redeemed us from our slavery to sin, and it was an even more beautiful act; *"For you know that it was not with perishable things such as silver or gold that you were redeemed from the empty way of life handed down to you from your forefathers, but with the precious blood of Christ, a lamb without blemish or defect." (1 Peter 1:18-19 NIV)*

Uncannily, hours after writing this, I opened my Bible to Isaiah 50. I was searching for a verse I thought was located in this chapter

70

of Isaiah. It wasn't, but the first two verses of Isaiah chapter 50 reinforced what I had just written. *This is what the LORD says: "Where is your mother's certificate of divorce with which I sent her away? Or to which of my creditors did I sell you? Because of your sins you were sold; because of your transgressions your mother was sent away. When I came, why was there no one? When I called, why was there no one to answer? Was my arm too short to ransom you? Do I lack the strength to rescue you?" (Isaiah 50:1-2 NIV)* Hosea prophesied to the northern kingdom of Israel, during the same time that Isaiah prophesied to the southern kingdom of Judah. They both dealt with the themes of rescue and redemption, using the concept of marriage to convey the reality of God's love for His people.

Turning now to my sister Laurie's assertion that most people reject the Gospel because they don't think God will forgive them for their sins. I want to take a moment to assure you that, unless you continue in rejection of the Gospel unto death, there is no sin too gross or committed too often to render you beyond the forgiveness of God. *"I tell you the truth, all the sins and blasphemies of men will be forgiven them." (Mark 3:28 NIV)* God desires to extend His grace and forgiveness to you. No one is too far gone. You simply have to repent and believe the Gospel.

Basics

"…Christ died for our sins according to the Scriptures, that he was buried, that **he was raised** *on the third day according to the Scriptures" (1 Corinthians 15:3-4 NIV* **emphasis added***)*

I N THIS SECTION, I want to briefly highlight a couple basic principles that are essential to biblical Christianity. I'll focus specifically on the resurrection because it is the most essential principle. I will also highlight the ascension because it follows closely in explaining the reality of the resurrection. If Christ is risen, where is He now?

The resurrection of Christ is a linchpin of the Gospel. For by it we know that the Father accepted the Son's sacrifice. Without it, we are lost. Our very salvation depends upon the historicity of the life, crucifixion, and the resurrection of Jesus. The apostle Paul testifies that *"…if Christ has not been raised, your faith is futile; you are still in your sins!" (1 Corinthians 15:17 NKJV)* Then Paul confidently writes, *"But in fact Christ has been raised from the dead, the firstfruits of those who have fallen asleep. For as by a man came death, by a man has come also the resurrection of the dead." (1 Corinthians 15:20-21 ESV)* In Romans 10:9 he states: *"That if you confess with your mouth, 'Jesus is Lord,' and* **believe in your heart that God raised him from the dead***, you will be saved." (NIV* **emphasis added***)* Our faith isn't simply to be placed in the historical reality of Christ; our faith is to be placed in a living Savior, Who was raised from the dead. This is a current reality, based on historical fact.

While giving his defense of the crucifixion and resurrection of Christ to King Agrippa, Paul was accused by Porcius Festus, the administrator over Judea, of being crazy, *"And as he was saying these things in his defense, Festus said with a loud voice, 'Paul, you are out of your mind; your great learning is driving you out of your mind.' But Paul said, 'I am not out of my mind, most excellent Festus, but I am speaking true and rational words. For the king knows about these things, and to him I speak boldly. For I am persuaded that none of these things has escaped his notice,* **for this has not been done in a corner.'"** *(Acts 26:24-26 ESV* **emphasis added***)*

The New Testament makes it explicit that the Gospel of Jesus Christ is based on eyewitness accounts.

"For what I received I passed on to you as of first importance: that Christ died for our sins according to the Scriptures, that he was buried, that he was raised on the third day according to the Scriptures, and that **he appeared to Peter, and then to the Twelve. After that, he appeared to more than five hundred of the brothers at the same time, most of whom are still living, though some have fallen asleep. Then he appeared to James, then to all the apostles,** *and last of all he appeared to me also, as to one abnormally born." (1 Corinthians 15:3-8 NIV* **emphasis added***)*

"That which was from the beginning, that which we have heard, that which we have seen with our eyes, that which we saw, and our hands touched, concerning the Word of life (and the life was revealed, and we have seen, and testify, and declare to you the life, the eternal life, which was with the Father, and was

revealed to us); that which we have seen and heard we declare to you, that you also may have fellowship with us. Yes, and our fellowship is with the Father, and with his Son, Jesus Christ." (1 John 1:1-3 WEB)

*"Many have undertaken to draw up an account of the things that have been fulfilled among us, just as they were handed down to us by those who from the first were **eyewitnesses** and servants of the word. Therefore, since I myself have carefully investigated everything from the beginning, it seemed good also to me to write an orderly account for you, most excellent Theophilus, so that you may know the certainty of the things you have been taught." (Luke 1:1-4 NIV* **emphasis added**)

Concerning the apostles, Luke writes *"After his suffering, he showed himself to these men and* **gave many convincing proofs that he was alive.** *He appeared to them over a period of forty days and spoke about the kingdom of God." (Acts 1:3 NIV* **emphasis added**)

The skeptic will say that I am using circular reasoning, using the Bible to prove the Bible; and as far as I have gone in this writing, they are correct. Moreover, some skeptics make the absurd claim that there aren't any non-Christian writers during the time of the birth and early growth of the church that collaborate the claims of Christianity. This is utter nonsense. There are many who didn't have a favorable opinion of Christianity. Amongst them are Flavius Josephus, Cornelius Tacitus, Pliny the younger, Celsus, Lucian, Epictectus, Emperor Marcus, and Porphyry.

In addition to this, Sir William Ramsey was a Scottish archaeologist who was skeptical of the New Testament accounts. Near the end of the 19th century, as a young historian, he set out to develop an independent historical/geographical study of first century Asia minor. He assumed that the Book of Acts was unreliable, which led him to ignore the account. However, the amount of usable historical information available was scant, so in desperation he turned to the Book of Acts. He was so astounded as to the accuracy of the book, that it led to his conversion to Christianity. He wrote, "Luke is a historian of the first rank; not merely are his statements trustworthy . . . this author should be placed along with the very greatest of historians"[12]

Indeed, for those who are able to set aside prejudice, they will find that the life, crucifixion, and resurrection of Jesus Christ are historical facts. *"Because it was not done in a corner,"* there is ample evidence upon which the truth of Christianity has been established. Many books have been written that display the evidence for Christianity. Books that I found helpful are *Evidence That Demands a Verdict* by Josh McDowell, *The Case for Christ* by Lee Strobel and *Cold-Case Christianity* by J. Warner Wallace.

Needless to say, it is not the purpose of my writing to give a rigorous defense of the historical accuracy of Christianity. It is my fear that many that are persistent in their unbelief have already put this book down. However, it is my prayer that they may still be reading, or that what they have read has caused the Holy Spirit to arouse a curiosity within that would inspire them to sincerely investigate the claims of Christ.

The final principle essential to Christianity is the Ascension of Jesus Christ; *"...he was taken up before their very eyes, and a cloud hid him from their sight." (Acts 1:9 NIV)* Paul's letters are amongst the earliest biblical documents. Probably the clearest reference to the ascension of Christ is found in Paul's letter to the church in Ephesus, written in A.D. 62. *"Therefore it says, 'When he ascended on high he led a host of captives, and he gave gifts to men.' (In saying, 'He ascended,' what does it mean but that he had also descended into the lower regions, the earth? He who descended is the one who also ascended far above all the heavens, that he might fill all things.)" (Ephesians 4:8-10 ESV)*

A theme that is established alongside the ascension is that of Jesus being seated at the right hand of God. Paul's letter to the church in Rome, written in A.D. 57, confirms this theme. *"It is Christ who died, yes rather, who was raised from the dead, who is at the right hand of God, who also makes intercession for us." (Romans 8:34 WEB)* Finally, Paul's first letter to the church in Thessalonica, written in A.D. 51, is the apostle's earliest known letter. It confirms that Christ is in heaven. *"...and to wait for his Son from heaven, whom he raised from the dead—Jesus, who delivers us from the coming wrath." (1 Thessalonians 1:10 WEB)*

It is quite widely accepted that Jesus was crucified sometime between A.D. 29-33. So then, working from the earliest date of A.D. 29, just 22 years after the crucifixion, we have written testimony by the apostle Paul from A.D. 51, confirming the resurrection and ascension of Christ. For his faith, Paul was tortured and then beheaded by the evil Emperor Nero in Rome, in A.D. 67.

I'll be the first one to admit that, taken on their face, the resurrection and ascension of Christ sound more like fantasy than fact. I mean it's a ridiculous story that transcends rationality. But the apostle Peter assures us; *"We did not follow cleverly invented stories when we told you about the power and coming of our Lord Jesus Christ, but we were **eyewitnesses** of his majesty." (2 Peter 1:16 NIV* **emphasis added***)* Rather than deny the faith, around A.D. 67, Peter was crucified upside down because he felt himself unworthy to be put to death in the same way as his Master. There is such a large amount of historical evidence that the resurrection can't be simply dismissed as fantasy. God challenges us to embrace the aforementioned as it truly is; supernatural fact.

An Assault on Pride by Faith

"For by grace you have been saved through faith, and that not of yourselves; it is the gift of God, not of works, that no one would boast." (Ephesians 2:8-9 WEB)

"God opposes the proud but gives grace to the humble." (James 4:6 & 1 Peter 5:5 NIV)

I PRAY THAT as you read through the previous sections you came to an understanding of the inability of sinful man to reconcile himself to a holy God, and that an age of grace was inaugurated through the death and resurrection of Jesus Christ. He is our substitute and representative before God. But His work must be appropriated; it must be received by faith.

Before I explain the concept of faith, I want to highlight several scriptures that clearly establish that salvation is by grace through faith alone. But first I'd like to introduce you to another concept; justification. Justification is the legal act where God declares a sinner to be innocent of his or her sins. It is not that the sinner is now sinless, but that he is "declared" sinless. This declaration of righteousness is what it means to be justified before God. A good way to relate the reality of justification is thinking it is just as if I'd (note the play on words, justified) never sinned.

Following is a sampling of verses about justification, faith and grace;

"For God so loved the world that he gave his one and only Son, that whoever believes in him shall not perish but have eternal life." (John 3:16 NIV) This well-known verse from the Gospel of John dovetails nicely with this passage from the first letter of John, *"By this God's love was revealed in us, that God has sent his one and only Son into the world that we might live through him. In this is love, not that we loved God, but that he loved us, and sent his Son as the atoning sacrifice for our sins." (1 John 4:9-10 WEB)*

"...being **justified freely by his grace** *through the redemption that is in Christ Jesus." (Romans 3:24 WEB* **emphasis added***)*

"Being therefore **justified by faith**, *we have peace with God through our Lord Jesus Christ." (Romans 5:1 WEB* **emphasis added***)*

"For Christ is the fulfillment of the law for righteousness **to everyone who believes.***" (Romans 10:1 WEB* **emphasis added***)*

"Know that a man is not justified by observing the law, but by faith in Jesus Christ. So we, too, have put our faith in Christ Jesus that we may be **justified by faith in Christ** *and not by observing the law, because by observing the law no one will be justified." (Galatians 2:16 NIV* **emphasis added***)*

"He redeemed us in order that the blessing given to Abraham might come to the Gentiles through Christ Jesus, so that **by faith** *we might receive the promise of the Spirit." (Galatians 3:14 NIV* **emphasis added***)*

"But the Scripture imprisoned everything under sin, so that the promise by faith in Jesus Christ might be given to those who believe. Now before faith came, we

*were held captive under the law, imprisoned until the coming faith would be revealed. So then, the law was our guardian until Christ came, in order that we might be **justified by faith**." (Galatians 3:22-24 ESV **emphasis added**)*

"And you also were included in Christ when you heard the word of truth, the Gospel of your salvation. Having believed, you were marked in him with a seal, the promised Holy Spirit," (Ephesians 1:13 NIV)

*"**For it is by grace you have been saved, through faith**—and this not from yourselves, it is the gift of God— not by works, so that no one can boast." (Ephesians 2:8-9 NIV **emphasis added**)*

*"And be found in him, not having a righteousness of my own, that which is of the law, but that which is **through faith in Christ**, the righteousness which is from God by faith." (Philippians 3:9 WEB **emphasis added**)*

*"…Holy Scriptures, which are able to make you wise for **salvation through faith** in Christ Jesus." (2 Timothy 3:15 NIV **emphasis added**)*

*"But when the kindness of God our Savior and his love toward mankind appeared, not by works of righteousness, which we did ourselves, but according to his mercy, he saved us, through the washing of regeneration and renewing by the Holy Spirit, whom he poured out on us richly, through Jesus Christ our Savior; that, **being justified by his grace**, we might be made heirs according to the hope of eternal life." (Titus 3:4-7 WEB **emphasis added**)*

"For Christ also suffered once for sins, the just for the unjust, that He might bring us to God, being put to death in the flesh but made alive by the Spirit." (1 Peter 3:18 NKJV)

The casual Bible reader might point to James 2:14-26 as contradictory to the principle of justification by faith alone. Specifically, James 2:24; *"You see then that a man is justified by works, and not by faith only." (NKJV)* But upon a closer look, James and Paul are not contradicting one another. Rather, their writings are complementary.

The works that James has in mind are the natural outward evidences of an inward reality. *"But someone will say, 'You have faith; I have deeds.' Show me your faith without deeds, and I will show you my faith by what I do." (James 2:18 NIV)* In other words, don't just talk the talk, walk the walk! James was trying to explain what real biblical faith is. It is not simply an intellectual acknowledgment or an emotional experience, but absolute trust and commitment to the Savior that expresses itself in the way we live.

The apostle Paul is in complete agreement with this principle. According to his writings, good works are the natural byproduct of genuine faith. We are not saved *by* good works, rather we are saved *for* good works. We have to guard against confusing the cause with the effect. Faith is the cause and works are the effect. We are saved by faith alone, but faith is never alone.

*"And God is able to make all grace abound to you, so that having all sufficiency in all things at all times, you may abound in **every good work.**" (2 Corinthians 9:8 ESV **emphasis added**)*

*"And we pray this in order that you may live a life worthy of the Lord and may please him in every way: bearing fruit in **every good work**, growing in the knowledge of God..." (Colossians 1:10 NIV **emphasis added**)*

"For by grace you have been saved through faith, and that not of yourselves; it is the gift of God, not of works, that no one would boast. For we are his workmanship, created in Christ Jesus **for good works**, *which God prepared before that we would walk in them." (Ephesians 2:8-10 WEB* **emphasis added***)*

"... **work out** *your own salvation with fear and trembling. For it is God who works in you both to will and to work, for his good pleasure." (Philippians 2:12b-13 WEB* **emphasis added***)* Notice the verse says to *"work out your salvation,"* not to work *for* your salvation. You cannot work out something you don't already have. In the larger context, this letter was written to the assembly of believers at Philippi. So *"your own"* does not refer to individual believers, but the church to which it was addressed. But even if we apply this verse to individual believers, we must accept the fact that the apostle was referring to sanctification and not salvation. I write about sanctification in **Becoming.**

"Now may our Lord Jesus Christ Himself, and our God and Father, who has loved us and given us everlasting consolation and good hope by grace, comfort your hearts and establish you in every **good word and work***." (2 Thessalonians 2:16-17 NKJV* **emphasis added***)*

"Therefore, if anyone cleanses himself from what is dishonorable, he will be a vessel for honorable use, set apart as holy, useful to the master of the house, ready for every **good work***. (2 Timothy 2:21 ESV* **emphasis added***)*

"Every Scripture is God-breathed and profitable for teaching, for reproof, for correction, and for instruction in righteousness, that the man of God may be complete, thoroughly equipped for every **good work***." (2 Timothy 3:16-17 WEB* **emphasis added***)*

*"They profess to know God, but in works they deny Him, being abominable, disobedient, and disqualified for every **good work**." (Titus 1:6 NKJV* **emphasis added**)

"For the grace of God that brings salvation has appeared to all men, teaching us that, denying ungodliness and worldly lusts, we should live soberly, righteously, and godly in the present age…" (Titus 2:11-12 NKJV)

*"…who gave Himself for us, that He might redeem us from every lawless deed and purify for Himself His own special people, **zealous for good works**." (Titus* 2:14 *NKJV* **emphasis added**)

*"This is a faithful saying, and these things I want you to affirm constantly, that those who have believed in God should be careful to **maintain good** works. These things are good and profitable to men." (Titus 3:8 NKJV* **emphasis added**)

*And let our people also learn to **maintain good** works, to meet urgent needs, that they may not be unfruitful." (Titus* 3:14 *NKJV* **emphasis added**)

Finally, *"Examine yourselves to see whether you are in the faith; test yourselves. Do you not realize that Christ Jesus is in you—unless, of course, you fail the test?" (2 Corinthians 13:5 NIV)*

The dictionary defines faith as "confidence or trust in a person or thing." In order to demonstrate the faith concept that is inherent to Christianity, I am going to borrow an analogy from another ministry; *Living Waters / The Way of the Master.*

Throughout my writing, I have intentionally compared our sin situation with *gravity*. Let's imagine that we are in an airplane about 2,500 feet above the earth. That's not much free fall time. At an unknown moment, we are going to be called to jump. Likewise, at an unknown moment, we will all be called to jump into eternity. *"...it is appointed for men to die once, and after this, judgment." (Hebrew 9:27 WEB)* But God has provided a parachute. Knowing that we will have to jump into eternity, we are called to *"put on the Lord Jesus Christ." (Romans 13:13 NKJV)*

The faith one would put in a parachute for his temporal life as he is called to jump from an airplane, is similar to the faith we are to put in Christ for our eternal life, as we are called to jump from the temporal into the eternal. We need to transfer any misplaced faith in our own goodness or good works (i.e. self-righteousness), religion, anyone or anything else, wholly in to Jesus Christ. He is our Savior! Many have grown up in the church and are riding the coat tails of their parent's faith. God doesn't have any grandchildren! We all have to make a choice to make the faith our own. It's not enough just to believe that the "parachute" exists. Rather, each individual must exercise faith in the "parachute" by putting it on and trusting completely in it. This faith is not something we can muster up, it is a gift that must be received. (cf. Ephesians 2:9)

I'm now going to transition to repentance. It seems appropriate, since faith and repentance are two sides of the same coin. You can't have one without the other. I discuss repentance in the section entitled **War**, but it is my understanding that there are two forms, or expressions of repentance communicated in the New Testament. *"Repent, then, and turn to God, so that your sins may be wiped out, that times of refreshing may come from the Lord..." (Acts 3:19 NIV)* Many, when presenting the Gospel, emphasize repentance before salvation.

"Repent and be saved!" But the idea of repentance unto salvation, in my view, has been distorted and misunderstood. In the Greek, the word repent means to change one's mind or way of thinking.

When God calls an unsaved man to repent, He means for that man to change his mind about how to reach God and to accept His way of salvation. *"...repentance toward God, and faith toward our Lord Jesus." (Acts 20:21 WEB)* The call is to redirect faith from self to the Savior. Therefore, this kind of repentance must include a change of mind concerning any misconceptions we have about God.

For the Jew, who had recently rejected Jesus, this meant realizing that God's righteousness, His righteous demands, surpass anything attainable by human effort. In Acts 3:19, quoted above, Peter called the Jews to change their mind about Who Jesus is, and embrace Him as their Savior and Messiah. *"For they being ignorant of God's righteousness, and seeking to establish their own righteousness, have not submitted to the righteousness of God." (Romans 10:3 NKJV)*

For the Gentile (i.e. the pagan) this meant recognizing God, the Lord of heaven and earth (cf. Acts 17:24) as the one true God, their Creator, resulting in their turning away from idolatry. *"They tell how you turned to God from idols to serve the living and true God, and to wait for his Son from heaven, whom he raised from the dead—Jesus, who rescues us from the coming wrath." (1 Thessalonians 1:9b-10 NIV)* For this first form of repentance to take place, our misconceptions and misperceptions of God must change. Our minds must change from any idea of saving ourselves through religion or good works, to trusting in Christ's death as payment for everything we have done wrong.

The second form of repentance, that I focus on later, is a change of mind that results in a change of behavior. This form flows naturally out of the first and takes place as we cooperate with the Spirit. This distinction is necessary because even the unsaved (i.e.

anyone who has not trusted Christ for salvation) have the ability to perform the second, but apart from the first there is no salvation. With regard to the second form of repentance, in a very real way, as we draw nearer to the Holy God, the Christian life ought to be one of continual repentance; though not a cycled repentance, where we are caught up in repenting for the same behavior.

It is my hope that you honestly evaluated yourself while reading **Bad News in the Mirror,** allowing you to appreciate the Gospel. If not, then the Gospel of grace through faith will stand as the ultimate assault on pride!

According to the principle of faith, God has disarmed mankind, whereby there will not be any boasting in heaven. *"Then what becomes of our boasting? It is excluded. By what kind of law? By a law of works? No, but by the law of faith. For we hold that one is justified by faith apart from works of the law." (Romans 3:27-28 ESV)* Why faith? Because *"...when a man works, his wages are not credited to him as a gift, but as an obligation." (Romans 4:4 NIV)* But *"Who has ever given to God, that God should repay him? For from him and through him and to him are all things. To him be the glory forever! Amen." (Romans 11:35-36 NIV)* To underscore this, remember that salvation is *"not of works, lest anyone should boast." (Ephesians 2:9 NKJV) "I don't make void the grace of God. For if righteousness is through the law, then Christ died for nothing!" (Galatians 2:21 WEB)*

Religion is one of mankind's chief sources of pride through which he boasts in himself. One deeply religious man who was confronted with the Gospel was Saul of Tarsus, later known as the apostle Paul. Based on personal experience, he recognized the uselessness of putting faith or confidence in the flesh. He wrote; *"If anyone else thinks he has reasons to put confidence in the flesh, I have more: circumcised on the eighth day, of the people of Israel, of the tribe of Benjamin, a*

Hebrew of Hebrews; in regard to the law, a Pharisee; as for zeal, persecuting the church; as for legalistic righteousness, faultless. But whatever was to my profit I now consider loss for the sake of Christ. What is more, I consider everything a loss compared to the surpassing greatness of knowing Christ Jesus my Lord, for whose sake I have lost all things. I consider them rubbish, that I may gain Christ and be found in him, not having a righteousness of my own that comes from the law, but that which is through faith in Christ—the righteousness that comes from God and is by faith." (Philippians 3:4-9 NIV)

When I write of religion, I have in mind mankind working to earn God's favor. In this sense, authentic Christianity is not a religion. It is a faith. In fact, Christianity is the only major "religion" that I am aware of that refers to itself as "the faith." The words "the faith" appear no less than 34 times in the New Testament.

It's not my intention here to parse the word "religion" or engage in semantics. I am simply explaining why I have written the way I have. I do not object to Christianity being called a religion in the broader sense of the term, but when someone asks me personally if I'm religious, I tell them "No, I'm a Christian." "While religion works to restrain our actions from the outside in, God always works from the inside out."[13] That's the indelible mark of Christianity; God in us, changing us.

One more thought before we move on. While it is not clearly revealed in Scripture, there is a plausible reason why God has chosen to redeem mankind by grace through faith rather than works. As you will see in the **Knowing Our Enemy** section, I write about how pride led to Satan's rebellion. God has already dealt with a proud creature; therefore, it is my contention that James 4:6 and 1 Peter 5:5 contain the most important attitude needed for salvation. *"God resists the proud but gives grace to the humble." (James 4:6 & 1 Peter 5:5 WEB)*

88

"Therefore humble yourselves under the mighty hand of God, that He may exalt you in due time." (1 Peter 5:6 NKJV)

Of Great Consequence

"He will punish those who do not know God and do not obey the Gospel of our Lord Jesus. They will be punished with everlasting destruction and shut out from the presence of the Lord and from the majesty of his power on the day he comes to be glorified in his holy people and to be marveled at among all those who have believed." (2 Thessalonians 1:8-10 NIV)

I PRAY THAT I have explained the beauty and truth of the Gospel adequately enough to enable you to make a clear decision. In this section, I hope to make clear the consequences of choosing wrongly. I won't mince words in this section. According to the Bible, the decision you make for or against Christ, whether to trust Him for your personal salvation, is of greatest consequence. Your decision will have eternal implications. Upon it hinges your eternal destiny – heaven or hell.

Many won't darken the door of a church because they assume that the pastor will be preaching hell-fire and brimstone. I've gone to many different churches over the years and I can honestly say that I've never once heard such a sermon preached there. In all sincerity, I don't believe that fear of hell ought to be our motivation for running to the Lord. His Love ought to be our motivation.

Jesus didn't warn us about hell to scare us. Rather, He warned us about a reality that we need to reckon with. "It is hardly ntary to God that we should choose Him as an alternative

t even this He accepts."[14]

s a vein of thinking today that denies the existence of hell, especially one that is eternal in nature. Honestly, my soul is also troubled by the prospect of an eternal hell for unbelievers and as much as I would like everybody to be saved, such a view is contrary to what the Bible reveals. No other biblical figure spoke more bluntly about the reality of hell than the Lord Jesus Christ. The words of Christ paint a picture of hell, that when meditated on, are quite disturbing, as they should be. It is to our own peril that we deny, ignore and make light of biblical warnings about hell. It is not necessary to take the language describing hell as literal. In fact, most scholars agree that the imagery is metaphorical (i.e. symbolic). But we also need to keep in mind that metaphors typically fall short of the reality they intend to describe.

The existence of hell is a staple doctrine or principle of biblical Christianity. Jesus taught that hell is a literal place, a place that was not intended for mankind. *"Then he will say also to those on the left hand, 'Depart from me, you cursed, into the eternal fire which is prepared for the devil and his angels." (Matthew 25:41 WEB)* When Adam chose to rebel against God, he committed the same sin as the devil and his angels – treason against high heaven! Although we bear the consequences of Adam's sin, being born spiritually dead in a fallen world, we will not be judged for his sin. According to Scripture, we will be judged by whether or not we receive Jesus' sacrifice on our behalf by putting our faith in Him.

"But the free gift isn't like the trespass. For if by the trespass of the one the many died, much more did the grace of God, and the gift by the grace of the one man, Jesus Christ, abound to the many. The gift is not as through one who sinned: for

*the judgment came by one to condemnation, but the free gift came of many trespasses to justification. For if by the trespass of the one, death reigned through the one; so much more will those **who receive** the abundance of grace and of the gift of righteousness reign in life through the one, Jesus Christ. So then as through one trespass, all men were condemned; even so through one act of righteousness, all men were justified to life." (Romans 5:15-18 WEB **emphasis added**)*

As I alluded to above, and as John Piper so elegantly wrote, "It's natural to want to believe in a God who saves all men no matter what they do or believe. But it is not biblical. Essential teachings of Scripture must be rejected in order to believe in such a God."[15] The teaching that all will be saved is known as Universalism. A particularly deceitful form of this teaching is Christian Universalism, which accurately maintains that Christ is the Savior and only way to God. However, it erroneously asserts that God has saved all through Christ, regardless of faith, or that He offers an infinite number of chances to repent and acknowledge the Gospel of Christ after death.

Scripture never concedes a second chance for sinners after death. The Bible is not silent on what happens after death. *"And as it is appointed for men to die once, but after this the judgment…"* (Hebrews 9:27 NKJV) Nevertheless, some popular writers and teachers do scriptural gymnastics in an effort to deny the reality and eternality of hell. They ultimately deny the plain meaning of scripture, the authority of God's word, and end up preaching another gospel, which Galatians 1:7-9 warns against.

"Evidently some people are throwing you into confusion and are trying to pervert the gospel of Christ. But even if we or an angel from heaven should preach a gospel other than the one we preached to you, let him be eternally condemned! As

we have already said, so now I say again: If anybody is preaching to you a gospel other than what you accepted, let him be eternally condemned"! (Galatians 1:7-9 NIV)

It's not my intent to disarm this false teaching in its entirety. Many books have been written that are helpful in exposing the fallacies of this teaching. Notwithstanding these, I will highlight several Scriptures that contradict Christian Universalism.

The fact that such teachings are so readily accepted in the church is due to a lack of discernment, which is due to scriptural ignorance. Writers, including me, can err or twist things by taking them out of context. For that reason, I encourage you to read and study the Bible for yourself. Scripture calls us to evaluate all teachings and discern truth from error; *"Test all things." (1 Thessalonians 5:21 WEB) "Beloved, don't believe every spirit, but test the spirits, whether they are of God, because many false prophets have gone out into the world." (1 John 4:1 WEB)* God's word is the standard by which we must evaluate all teachings.

Regarding hell; *"Many of those who sleep in the dust of the earth shall awake, some to everlasting life, and some to shame and everlasting contempt." (Daniel 12:2 WEB)* Taken in context, the word everlasting means forever, always or eternal, for in verse 7 of the same passage, the same Hebrew word is used in reference to the eternal God. *"I heard the man clothed in linen, who was above the waters of the river, when he held up his right hand and his left hand to heaven, and swore by him who lives* **forever…***" (Daniel 12:7 WEB* **emphasis added***)*

Daniel 12:2 parallels nicely with Matthew 25:41 and 46; *"Then he will say to those on his left, 'Depart from me, you who are cursed, into the eternal fire prepared for the devil and his angels.' …Then they will go away to eternal punishment, but the righteous to eternal life." (NIV)* The punishment is eternal in the same way that the life is eternal. Essentially, those who deny the existence of an eternal hell, forfeit the right to believe in an eternal heaven!

One key verse that deserves attention is Colossians 1:20, a favorite verse used by many Universalists: *"and through him (Jesus) to reconcile to himself all things, whether things on earth or things in heaven, by making peace through his blood, shed on the cross.'"* (NIV) They teach that all things include mankind. However, this verse does not teach a universal salvation. Rather, it presents the scope, goal, and means of reconciliation. The scope of reconciliation extends not just to human beings but to all of creation which was affected by sin. Romans 8:20-22 says, *"For the creation was subjected to frustration, not by its own choice, but by the will of the one who subjected it, in hope that the creation itself will be liberated from its bondage to decay and brought into the glorious freedom of the children of God. We know that the whole creation has been groaning as in the pains of childbirth right up to the present time."* (NIV)

The physical world was affected by sin, not by its choice but by the choice of Adam. Christ's victory over sin restored order over creation by bringing it again under His lordship, and full restoration will take place in the future.

Angels and human beings, unlike the material world, have a choice. Reconciliation involves two parties who voluntarily decide to make peace. Fallen angels knowingly rebelled against Christ and reconciliation is not possible. Humans also must make a choice to receive God's invitation through Christ or to reject it. This is made clear in the following verses:

95

"Once you were alienated from God and were enemies in your minds because of your evil behavior. But now he has reconciled you by Christ's physical body through death to present you holy in his sight, without blemish and free from accusation— **if you continue in your faith, established and firm, not moved from the hope held out in the Gospel.** *This is the Gospel that you heard and that has been proclaimed to every creature under heaven, and of which I, Paul, have become a servant." (Colossians 1:21-23 NIV* **emphasis added***)* Paul states that we were once *"alienated"* from God and we are reconciled *"if indeed you continue in the faith . . . not shifting from the hope of the gospel."* The reconciliation depends on the believer receiving Christ by faith and persevering in that faith. Numerous other verses make faith in Christ necessary for reconciliation (Jn. 3:18, 5:24; Rom. 1:17; 3:21-26).[16]

Do not misunderstand, it is not that our continuance in faith earns us reconciliation. Rather, it is by continuance that the reality of our faith is proven. *"They went out from us, but they were not of us; for if they had been of us, they would have continued with us; but they went out that they might be made manifest, that none of them were of us." (1 John 2:19 NKJV)*

I would agree with the Christian Universalist in the sense that reconciliation through the atoning blood of Christ is unlimited, or available to all. Christ died for all. *"And he is the atoning sacrifice for our sins, and not for ours only, but also for the whole world." (1 John 2:2 WEB)* But Scripture is clear that while God has made the provision of salvation for all mankind, it is effective only for those who choose to repent and believe. *"Whoever believes in the Son has eternal life, but whoever rejects the Son will not see life, for God's wrath remains on him." (John 3:36 NIV)*

If hell were a temporary remedial place like a purgatory, as many of these writers' assert, Jesus would not have taught that there is a sin that will not be forgiven: *"Therefore I tell you, every sin and blasphemy will be forgiven men, but the blasphemy against the Spirit will not be forgiven men. Whoever speaks a word against the Son of Man, it will be forgiven him; but whoever speaks against the Holy Spirit, it will not be forgiven him, neither in this age, nor in that which is to come." (Matthew 12:31-32 WEB)* "If hell is to be emptied at some point, all sin would have to be forgiven. But Jesus teaches that there is sin that will never be forgiven."[17]

Prior to the statement in Matthew 12:31-32, in Matthew 12:24 the Pharisees had accused Jesus of casting out spirits by Beelzebub (i.e. Satan). So it would seem according to the context, blasphemy of the Holy Spirit is attributing the work of the Holy Spirit to Satan.

A continuous refusal to listen to the convicting voice of the Holy Spirit leads to sin and a hardening of the heart. *"So I tell you this, and insist on it in the Lord, that you must no longer live as the Gentiles* (pagans) *do, in the futility of their thinking. They are darkened in their understanding and* **separated from the life of God** *because of the ignorance that is in them due to* **the hardening of their hearts. Having lost all sensitivity, they have given themselves over to sensuality so as to indulge in every kind of impurity, with a continual lust for more."** *(Ephesians 4:17-19 NIV* **emphasis added)** The heart can become so hard that it is no longer capable of responding to God.

Even so, God patiently and continually offers us the gift of repentance. *"The Lord is not slow concerning his promise, as some count slowness; but is patient with us, not wishing that any should perish, but that all should come to repentance." (2 Peter 3:9 WEB)* But whatever spiritual state a person is in when he dies, he will be in that state for all eternity.

Changing gears for a moment, as promised in **The Real Triumph,** I would now like to elaborate on a common misconception propagated by the world, that "we are all children of God." Scripture is clear that God loves all of His image bearers, however, being a child of God is a privilege shared only by believers in Christ. There are many Scripture passages that indicate this; *"But as many as received him, to them he gave the right to become God's children, to those who believe in his name." (John 1:12 WEB) "This means that it is not the children of the flesh who are the children of God, but the children of the promise are counted as offspring." (Romans 9:8 ESV) "You are all sons of God* **through faith** *in Christ Jesus." (Galatians 3:26 NIV* **emphasis added***)*

Indeed, Jesus called some children of "the devil!" *"You are of your father the devil…" (John 8:44 ESV)* The apostles John, Matthew and Paul expand on this; *"This is how we know who the children of God are and who the* **children of the devil** *are: Anyone who does not do what is right is not a child of God; nor is anyone who does not love his brother." (1 John 3:10 NIV* **emphasis added***)* "*…the tares are the sons of the wicked one. The enemy who sowed them is the devil." (Matthew 13:38-39 NKJV)* "*…were by nature children of wrath." (Ephesians 2:3 NKJV)*

This is why, in his conversation with Nicodemus, Jesus stressed the importance of being born again; *"Truly, truly, I say to you, unless one is born again he cannot see the kingdom of God." (John 3:3 ESV) "Truly, truly, I say to you, unless one is born of water and the Spirit, he cannot enter the kingdom of God." (John 3:5 ESV)* Being born again is a spiritual rebirth, by which we become children of God. Since the concept of water baptism for repentance had already been introduced in Scripture, many interpret water in the previous verse as referring to water baptism. I disagree. While I do see a baptism in this passage, it is not of water, but rather of the Spirit.

I believe that the water in this passage refers to that which happens prior to physical birth. The breaking of the amniotic sac and the water – like fluid that gushes forth, signals that the baby is about to be born. This interpretation is supported by the immediate context: *"Most assuredly, I say to you, unless one is born again, he cannot see the kingdom of God.' ⁴ Nicodemus said to Him, 'How can a man be born when he is old? Can he enter a second time into his mother's womb and be born?' ⁵ Jesus answered, 'Most assuredly, I say to you, unless one is born of water and the Spirit, he cannot enter the kingdom of God. ⁶ That which is born of the flesh is flesh, and that which is born of the Spirit is spirit.'"* (John 3:3-6 NKJV)

As we look at verse 4 above, we see that Nicodemus relates the words of Jesus with physical birth and asks, *"How can a man be born when he is old? Can he enter a second time into his mother's womb, and be born?"* (John 3:4 WEB) In John 3:5 Jesus makes it clear that he is referring to a spiritual birth as he explains the necessity of two different kinds of birth, contrasted by water and the Spirit. *"Unless one is born of water and the Spirit, he cannot enter the kingdom of God."* (John 3:5 ESV) As if to further clarify His statement, He says *"That which is born of the flesh is flesh. That which is born of the Spirit is spirit."* (John 3:6 WEB) I'd further argue that in John 3:5 Jesus excludes fallen angels from the kingdom of God (cf. Hebrews 2:16) and limits salvation to the realm of mankind, those born of water.

I realize that this interpretation of John 3:5 will be unique to most, and while I believe it is correct, you don't have to agree. I'm just putting it out there for you to prayerfully consider.

I do not mean to diminish water baptism as an act of obedience to the Lord. Water baptism is an outward expression of an inward reality; it is a command given to believers as public evidence of their conversion, not as a means of salvation. There are many Scriptures that bare this out.

One example is Acts 10:43-48, which recounts that those in Cornelius' house, who heard Peter preaching, were baptized with the

Holy Spirit prior to their water baptism. *"'All the prophets testify about him, that through his name everyone who **believes** in him will receive remission of sins.' While Peter was still speaking these words, the Holy Spirit fell on all those who heard the word. They of the circumcision who believed were amazed, as many as came with Peter, because the gift of the Holy Spirit was also poured out on the Gentiles. For they heard them speaking in other languages and magnifying God. Then Peter answered, 'Can anyone forbid these people from being baptized with water? They have received the Holy Spirit just like us.' He commanded them to be baptized in the name of Jesus Christ. Then they asked him to stay some days."* (WEB **emphasis added)**

Upon his recounting of the previous events to the Hebrew church in Jerusalem, Peter explained, "I remembered the word of the Lord, how he said, *John indeed baptized in water, but you will be baptized in the Holy Spirit.'"* (Acts 11:16 WEB) Holy Scripture reveals that these believers were baptized by the Spirit into the church, the body of Christ, by faith. *"For we were all baptized by one Spirit into one body—whether Jews or Greeks, slave or free—and we were all given the one Spirit to drink."* (1 Corinthians 12:13 NIV)

I could go on, but this is a point of contention within Christendom. It's not my desire to trip you up, but rather to challenge you to search these things out for yourself. I also realize that there is a tendency to read Scripture through the prism of the denomination that we identify with. Nevertheless, I encourage you to look past your denominational prism and be open to the Word of God.

Many claim that a God of love would never send anyone to hell. But I contend that it is precisely because of love that God allows people to reject Him and choose hell. As I wrote in **The Beginning of Romance,** love that is forced upon another is not love at all. God does not force Himself on anyone. To do so would be tantamount to rape by the Deity. God is the perfect gentleman; *"Behold, I stand at the door and knock. If anyone hears my voice and opens the door, then I will come in to him, and will dine with him, and he with me."* (Revelation 3:20 WEB) God invites us to know Him and He desires us to accept the gift of salvation, but He honors our choice to reject Him because this is the essence of love.

With the doctrine of hell, God's just nature isn't diminished, as some contend. Rather, it is established. Let's think this through. Fallen mankind has set up judgments or measures of justice for criminals or lawbreakers. How much greater is God's justice made known in that He judges sin, which has been committed against Himself. Yet, for those who are reconciled with God, through Christ's sacrifice, eternal judgment has passed over. Christ is our Passover!

Many object to the exclusive nature of the Christian faith. Rather than thanking God that He has provided the Way, I have heard it uttered, "Why would God have provided only one way to heaven?" While this may be a legitimate question, in most cases the people who ask this question aren't looking for an answer. For as the question implies, they have already answered it themselves and they use it to justify their rejection of the Gospel. We are all rebels and some refuse to lay down their arms because they cannot wrap their finite minds around an infinite God. It comes down to pride.

Concerning the exclusivity of Christianity, a common assertion is that all roads (i.e. religions) lead to God. But all the major world religions make absolute truth claims regarding the way to salvation. For example, Hindus claim that salvation (liberation) is achieved when a person transcends this world of illusion by building up enough positive karma or good works to escape the cycle of reincarnation. Buddhists say that salvation (Nirvana) is the result of detaching one's self from the desires of the physical, material world. Islam states that the possibility of salvation results from submitting one's life to Allah and carrying out the Five Pillars of Islam. In contrast, Christianity proclaims that salvation comes by grace through faith in Jesus Christ. It would be an absurdity and an affront to deny the uniqueness of these religions and claim that they all lead to God. Since their claims are contrary to one another, one of these religions is true or none of them are true, but logically they cannot all be true at the same time. To claim otherwise is to violate the Law of Non-Contradiction. [18]

Even though I have the wherewithal to do so, it is not my intention or purpose to delve into the differences between Christianity and other world religions, but let me provide a summary of the biggest differences. The most basic difference is that all other religions are based on human efforts to reach God or a superior state of being. People are trying to attain something with the hope of living a better life and/or gaining eternal life. Whereas, in Christianity God reached down to humanity to bring them into relationship with Himself. Salvation is free gift, which we accept by faith in Jesus Christ, Who, out of love, offered Himself as a sacrifice for our sins, so that we can be in right standing with God.

Additionally, the founders of other religions were fallible human beings, who are dead. However, the founder of Christianity is alive. Not only is Jesus seated at the right hand of God (Colossians 3:1), He also dwells within the hearts of His children (Ephesians 3:17), transforming us from the inside out.

"Do you think that I have come to give peace in the earth? I tell you, no, but rather division." *(Luke 12:51 WEB)* Jesus Christ continues to be the most controversial and divisive figure in history. Most people accept that Jesus was a good moral teacher. But from where did they get that idea? Most got the idea from the Bible, and yet they reject the plain teaching of the Bible that Jesus was more than just a good moral teacher – much more. One cannot logically accept part of a testimony and reject the rest. One must accept it all or reject it all. Therefore, all of the words and miracles of Jesus found in the Bible ought to carry equal weight. Otherwise we find ourselves with *"another Jesus"* *(2 Corinthians 11:4 WEB)*. It is neither popular nor politically correct, but Jesus' words clearly teach the exclusive, one-way nature of salvation. *"I am the way, the truth, and the life. No one comes to the Father except through me."* *(John 14:6 WEB)* And this truth is not isolated to this one text, as the following references demonstrate;

"Enter in by the narrow gate; for wide is the gate and broad is the way that leads to destruction, and many are those who enter in by it." *(Matthew 7:13 WEB)*

"Whoever believes and is baptized will be saved, but whoever does not believe will be condemned." *(Mark 16:16 ESV)*

"Whoever believes in him is not condemned, but whoever does not believe stands condemned already because he has not believed in the name of God's one and only Son." *(John 3:18 NIV)*

"I said therefore to you that you will die in your sins; for unless you believe that I am he, you will die in your sins." *(John 8:24 WEB)*

"There is salvation in none other, for neither is there any other name under heaven, that is given among men, by which we must be saved!" (Acts 4:12 WEB)

"For there is one God, and one mediator between God and men, the man Christ Jesus." (1 Timothy 2:5 WEB)

A common question raised is about those who have never had the opportunity to hear the Gospel. This is a legitimate question, but like the previous question, many use it as an excuse to reject the Gospel. If they were truly concerned about those who have never heard, they would do everything in their power to see that everyone heard the Gospel message. But Scripture is clear, "Men will be judged by the light that they have had, not by the light they never knew." [19] John Piper, with whom Scripture agrees on this issue, conveyed that for those who have not heard the gospel, judgment will be based on their failure to acknowledge God as He reveals Himself in creation and in their conscience. [20]

"And that servant who knew his master's will, and did not prepare himself or do according to his will, shall be beaten with many stripes. But he who did not know, yet committed things deserving of stripes, shall be beaten with few. For everyone to whom much is given, from him much will be required; and to whom much has been committed, of him they will ask the more." (Luke 12:47-48 NKJV)

"For since the creation of the world His invisible attributes are clearly seen, being understood by the things that are made, even His eternal power and Godhead, so that they are without excuse, because although they knew God, they did not glorify Him as God, nor were thankful, but became futile in their thoughts, and their foolish hearts were darkened." (Romans 1:20-21 NKJV)

104

"(for when Gentiles who don't have the law do by nature the things of the law, these, not having the law, are a law to themselves, in that they show the work of the law written in their hearts, their conscience testifying with them, and their thoughts among themselves accusing or else excusing them) in the day when God will judge the secrets of men, according to my Good News, by Jesus Christ." (Romans 2:14-16 WEB)

According to Scripture, even though God's love and justice are established in allowing people to go to hell, He does not take pleasure in it. *"Do I take any pleasure in the death of the wicked? Declares the Sovereign LORD. Rather, am I not pleased when they turn from their ways and live?"* (Ezekiel 18:23 NIV) As I wrote earlier, God patiently and continually offers us the gift repentance. *"The Lord...is longsuffering toward us, not willing that any should perish but that all should come to repentance."* (2 Peter 3:9 NKJV) In Luke 19:41-44, we see the heart of God breaking over the rejection of His people; *"As he approached Jerusalem and saw the city, he wept over it and said, 'If you, even you, had only known on this day what would bring you peace—but now it is hidden from your eyes...because you did not recognize the time of God's coming to you.'"* (NIV) Do not miss the time of God's coming to you!

"Behold, now is the favorable time; behold, now is the day of salvation." (2 Corinthians 6:2 ESV) There is a choice you must make and to choose not to choose is in fact a choice. Or put more succinctly; indecision is a decision. Jesus said, *"He who is not with me is against me, and he who does not gather with me, scatters."* (Matthew 12:30 WEB) With that statement He drew the proverbial line in the sand of eternity.

Finally, believers need not fear hell. Having accepted the gift of salvation, we can and should know our eternal destination. *"These things I have written to you who believe in the name of the Son of God, **that*** *you may know that you have eternal life, and that you may continue to believe in the name of the Son of God." (1 John 5:13 WEB* **emphasis added***)* We can have assurance that we have been delivered; *"And it is God who establishes us with you in Christ, and has anointed us, and who has also put his seal on us and given us his Spirit in our hearts as a guarantee." (2 Corinthians 1:20-21 ESV)*

Some might think it's arrogant to be so sure that we have eternal life, and it would be if we were relying on our own goodness or merit. But we aren't. We are fully convinced of our spiritual bankruptcy and that Jesus has given us eternal life, not because of what we've done, but because of what He did. Finally, fear ought not to be a motivating factor for Christians, but faith that is made perfect through the love of God in Christ Jesus. *"There is no fear in love. But perfect love drives out fear, because fear has to do with punishment. The one who fears is not made perfect in love." (1 John 4:18 NIV)*

Now you might ask me where I think my loved ones who have died ended up. Honestly, I don't know. I definitely hope with all that is in me that they are in heaven, but I am not God. I am unable to evaluate where any individual stands in their relationship with Him. Ultimately, we must trust God to do what is right. *"Shall not the Judge of the earth do what is just?" (Genesis 18:25 ESV)*

No matter where our loved ones ended up eternally, I guarantee that their desire is for us to embrace Christ and spend eternity in heaven. This fact is evident as one reads the account of Lazarus and the Rich Man, found in Luke 16:19-31. In this passage, Jesus pulled back the curtain on the eternal states of two men. Lazarus was a poor man, who languished outside the unnamed rich man's gate. Meanwhile, the rich man ignored Lazarus' plight and enjoyed the luxury obtained through his riches.

Both men die. Lazarus goes to paradise and the rich man goes to hades. The rich man pleads with Abraham concerning his torment. After recognizing the justice of his situation, he turns his attention to his loved ones. *"He said, 'I ask you therefore, father, that you would send him* (Lazarus) *to my father's house; for I have five brothers, that he may testify to them, so they won't also come into this place of torment.' But Abraham said to him, 'They have Moses and the prophets. Let them listen to them.' He said, 'No, father Abraham, but if one goes to them from the dead, they will repent.' He said to him, 'If they don't listen to Moses and the prophets, neither will they be persuaded if one rises from the dead.'"* *(Luke 16:27-31 WEB)*

That said, I'll end this section with a poem that is revealing and encourages humility.

I was shocked, confused, bewildered
As I entered Heaven's door,
Not by the beauty of it all,
Nor the lights or its decor.

But it was the folks in Heaven
Who made me sputter and gasp--
The thieves, the liars, the sinners,
The alcoholics and the trash.

There stood the kid from seventh grade
Who swiped my lunch money twice.
Next to him was my old neighbor
Who never said anything nice.

Ed, who I always thought

Was rotting away in hell,
Was sitting pretty on cloud nine,
Looking incredibly well.

I nudged Jesus, "What's the deal?
I would love to hear Your take.
How'd all these sinners get up here?
God must've made a mistake.

"And why is everyone so quiet,
So somber – give me a clue."
"Hush, child," He said,
"They're all in shock.
No one thought they'd be seeing you."
(Author unknown)

Who I Am

Therefore, if anyone is in Christ, he is a new creation; the old has gone, the new has come! (2 Corinthians 5:17 NIV)

NOT LONG AFTER my conversion, which took place while watching a televangelist from my hospital bed at home about a year after the crash, I began to learn who I am in Christ. An instrumental part of this was what I learned when my parents and I started attending a bi-weekly Bible study hosted by our friends Greg and Karen, and lead by Tom, who at that time was the pastor of Immanuel Church in Roseville Michigan. Growing up Catholic, if I read the Bible, I read it with blinders on. One night I remarked to Greg that Revelation 5:8, *"…and golden bowls full of incense, which are the prayers of the saints." (WEB),* was evidence that saints pray for us.

Catholics and most in Christendom today, believe saints to be exceptionally holy people, whom, after they pass into glory, are canonized by the church and recognized as saints. Using the Word of God, Pastor Tom made the argument that the word *saint* was a common word used to refer to any ordinary believer in Christ. Note that in Scripture it always appears in the plural form; saints. *"To the church of God which is at Corinth, to those who are **sanctified** in Christ Jesus, called **to be saints…**" (1 Corinthians 1:2 NKJV **emphasis added**)* The word sanctified is used first, which literally means "to be made holy." There really isn't much difference between the words sanctified, and saints or holy ones, or literally, "set apart ones." We are sanctified and we are called to be saints. Pastor Tom drove home his point by accentuating the fact that the Corinthian church, to whom the letter was addressed, was one of the most immature, carnal congregations known in the New Testament writings.

First off, I ought to clarify that a church is not a building, but rather a body of believers. The Corinthian church divided itself into groups, with each group lifting up their leader as being superior to the others (1 Corinthians 1:10-17). There was sexual immorality in the church (5:1-11, 6:15-16), they abused the Lord's Supper (11:17-22), and overemphasized the spiritual gift of tongues (14:1-24). They had problems, many of which I haven't cited. Most of these problems were a result of pride. Needless to say, these believers were not what one would think of when the word 'saints' comes to mind. Within Paul's first letter to the church at Corinth was a call to repent of such worldliness and to live up to the calling they received. Still, he didn't shy away from calling them saints.

Like the Bereans of Acts 17:11, I examined the Scriptures to see if this was true. What I discovered solidified Pastor Tom's argument. The word 'saints' appears no less than 44 times in the New Testament and with the exception of a few verses, like in Revelation 5:8, where I stumbled in my interpretation, the word clearly refers to believers in Christ, living on the earth. For example, saints have needs (Romans 12:13), there were poor among them (Romans 15:26), they were ministered to, i.e. their needs were met (2 Corinthians 8:4), they were prayed for (Ephesians 6:8), they were greeted (Romans 6:15), and sent greetings (2 Corinthians 13:13).

Years later, upon further study, I learned that the words *"to be,"* which appear in 1 Corinthians 1:2 (refer above) are absent in the original Greek. So the verse could literally be read *"To the church of*

God which is at Corinth, to those who are sanctified in Christ Jesus, called **saints...**" (NKJV **emphasis added**) However, when reading the Greek, the inference "*to be*" is usually made. Note that this same inference is made in 1 Corinthians 1:1; "*Paul, called* **to be** *an apostle of Christ Jesus through the will of God.*" (WEB **emphasis** added) So observe that they were called saints in the same way that Paul was called an apostle, which was by divine call. We do not become saints by acting in a saintly way. Rather, because we are saints we should manifest saintliness.

"**To the saints** *in Ephesus, the faithful in Christ Jesus.*" (Ephesians 1:1 NIV **emphasis added**)

So I learned that I am a saint. I could definitely deal with that!

On another evening, Pastor Tom presented another study that rocked my identity. He basically asked us what we thought God saw when He looked at us. Did He see our sin? Well, it seemed to me that an all-knowing, all-seeing God would obviously see our sinfulness. But using 2 Corinthians 5:21, Pastor Tom taught that if we are in Christ, God sees His only Son, He sees us as His own righteousness. 2 Corinthians 5:21 reads, "*God made him who had no sin to be sin for us, so that in him we might become the righteousness of God.*" (NIV) I could've gotten hung up on the words *might become*. But I was there to learn, not argue. I would put the teaching to the test by examining the Scriptures later.

My findings partially established Pastor Tom's assertion. It's not as though God cannot see our sin. In fact, He does. Scripture clearly reveals that God disciplines those He loves. "*Those whom I love I reprove and discipline.*" (Revelation 3:19 ESV) Also see 1 Corinthians

11:32 and Hebrews 12:5-10. The discipline of God implies the necessity of seeing sin done by believers. Nevertheless, one of the verses that I also keyed in on was 1 Corinthians 1:30; *"It is because of him that you are in Christ Jesus, who has become for us wisdom from God—that is,* **our righteousness, holiness and redemption.***" (NIV* **emphasis added)** Therefore, if we are in Christ, He is our righteousness, our holiness, and our redemption. We are no longer defined by our sins. (cf. 1 Corinthians 6:9-11) It is not our sin that God identifies us with, but Jesus' righteousness. We are legally righteous. *"This righteousness from God comes through faith in Jesus Christ to all who believe." (Romans 3:22 NIV)*

So I learned that I am the righteousness of God in Christ Jesus!

This understanding shed new light on the Gospel of Jesus Christ. I now saw that when someone comes to trust in Christ there is an exchange. Our sin is transferred or imputed to Christ and Christ's righteousness is imputed to us. In other words, not only are our sins forgiven, which is good news in and of itself, but we also receive a righteousness that is not our own. This exchange is a mind blowing, game changing, life altering reality. But I was just beginning to understand my new identity.

In the section **War,** I refer to Neil Anderson's book *The Bondage Breaker,* and how helpful it was to me during that time. In *The Bondage Breaker,* Anderson referred to another book he wrote entitled *Victory Over the Darkness.* Since *The Bondage Breaker* had been so helpful, I decided to check out *Victory Over the Darkness.*

Victory Over the Darkness was another key in helping me discover my identity in Christ. I learned that the two most essential elements to living a victorious life are (1) knowing God and (2) knowing who we are in Christ. My inspiration for the following list came from *Victory Over the Darkness*. While this list contains many of the same references and concepts in Anderson's book, it will also contain many not cited by him, as well as omissions. I wanted to create my own list, rather than just copy Anderson's. Obviously, this list isn't exhaustive. I encourage you to read through it out loud and often until it becomes a part of you. Even then, we need periodic reminders to sustain our identity. This is part of the transformation by the renewing of our minds to which we are called. *"Don't be conformed to this world, but* **be transformed by the renewing of your mind.**" *(Romans 12:2 WEB* **emphasis added)**

Who I Am in Christ

I am salt and light to the world (Matthew 5:14-16)
I am Christ's brother (Matthew 12:50)
I am a friend of Christ's (John 15:15)
I have peace with God through Jesus Christ (Romans 5:1)
I have been reconciled with God (Romans 5:10)
I reign in life through Christ (Romans 5:17)
I was crucified with Christ (Romans 6:6)
I am no longer a slave to sin (Romans 6:6)
I am dead to sin, but alive to God in Christ Jesus (Romans 6:11)
I have been set free from sin (Romans 6:17)
I am not condemned (Romans 8:1)
I am an heir of God – a co-heir with Christ (Romans 8:17)
I am assured that all things work together for good (Romans 8:28)
I am more than a conqueror (Romans 8:37)
I have been sanctified in Christ Jesus (1 Corinthians 1:2)
I am righteous, holy and redeemed in Christ (1 Corinthians 1:30)

I have been washed, sanctified and justified (1 Corinthians 6:11)

I am a member of Christ (1 Corinthians 6:15)

I am a temple of the Holy Spirit (1 Corinthians 6:19)

I am not my own, I was bought at a price, I belong to God (1 Corinthians 6:19-20)

I am the fragrance of Christ unto God (2 Corinthians 2:15)

I am a letter from Christ (2 Corinthians 3:3)

I have been given the Spirit as a deposit (2 Corinthians 5:5)

I am a new creation in Christ, the old has gone, the new has come (2 Corinthians 5:17)

I am Christ's ambassador (2 Corinthians 5:20)

I am *becoming* the righteousness of God in Christ Jesus (2 Corinthians 5:21)

I am a temple of the living God (2 Corinthians 6:16)

I have been crucified with Christ, it is no longer I who live, but Christ who lives in me (Galatians 2:20)

I am a child of Abraham (Galatians 3:7)

I am a son of God (Galatians 3:26)

I have crucified the sinful nature with its passions and desires (Galatians 5:24)

I am a saint (Ephesians 1:1)

I have been blessed with every spiritual blessing in the heavenly realms (Ephesians 1:3)

I have been marked in Christ with a seal, the promised Holy Spirit (Ephesians 1:13)

I have been raised up with Christ and I am seated with Him in the heavenly realms (Ephesians 2:6)

I am God's workmanship (Ephesians 2:10)

I am confident that God will complete the good work He has begun in me (Philippians 1:6)

I am a partaker of grace (Philippians 1:7)

I am a citizen of heaven (Philippians 3:20)

I can do (noting the context, this should be read as endure) all things through Christ who strengthens me (Philippians 4:13)

I am a partaker of the inheritance of the saints in the light (Colossians 1:12)

I have been delivered from the power of darkness and conveyed into the kingdom of the Son (Colossians 1:13)

I am complete in Him (Colossians 2:10)

I am hidden with Christ in God (Colossians 3:3)

I have taken off my old self and I have put on the new self, who is renewed in knowledge according to the image of my Creator (Colossians 3:9-10)

I am one of God's chosen people, holy and dearly loved (Colossians 3:12)

I am a child of light and a child of the day, I do not belong to the night or darkness (1 Thessalonians 5:5)

I have not been given a spirit of fear, but of power, love, and a sound mind (2 Timothy 1:7)

I am a partaker of a heavenly calling (Hebrews 3:1)

I am a partaker of Christ (Hebrews 3:14)

I have been sanctified (Hebrews 10:10)

I have been perfected (Hebrews 10:14)

I am part of a chosen people, a royal priesthood, a holy nation, a people belonging to God (1 Peter 2:9)

I have an anointing from the Holy One (1 John 2:20)

I am a child of God (1 John 3:1)

I have overcome the world (1 John 5:5)

Accepting my identity in Christ completely revolutionized my life. God was calling me to another level. We cannot live beyond what we perceive ourselves to be. *"For as he thinks in his heart, so is he." (Proverbs 23:7 NIV)* Christians are fond of saying, "I'm just a sinner saved by grace." In keeping with the Proverbs 23:7 line of thought, losers lose, failures fail, and sinners sin. While it's true that we were sinners and we were saved by grace, the Gospel is so transformative that we are challenged to completely disavow our old nature. The glory of the Gospel is that we are no longer sinners. Rather, we are saints who sin. We are saints because that's what God calls us, and we sin because we are still in the flesh. This is not mere positive thinking. This is accepting truth and rejecting lies.

The world and the devil beat us down with lies. The main strategy of Satan is to distort the character of God and the truth of who we are. When we accept his lies as reality we will live accordingly. Many have been so beaten down and brutalized with words that the process of renewing your mind will be difficult. The world has it backwards. It is not what we do that determines who we are; it is who we are that determines what we do.

I was beginning to become who I am in Christ. Because of my new identity, when I knowingly sin I get very uncomfortable, because it's inconsistent with who I perceive myself to be. This is because "we cannot consistently behave in a way that is inconsistent with how we perceive ourselves, nor can our feelings about ourselves be any different from our perceptions about ourselves."[21] My response to sin is to confess it to God, repent and move forward. I hold on to this promise; *"If we confess our sins, he is faithful and just to forgive us our sins and to cleanse us from all unrighteousness." (1 John 1:9 ESV)*

In social psychology, there is a theory called cognitive dissonance that seeks to explain this phenomenon. Laying aside the psychological jargon, cognitive dissonance is the discomfort which comes with holding two conflicting thoughts in the mind at the same time. The discomfort is the tension between the opposing thoughts. To release this tension, we can take one of three actions. The first, and the most appropriate action when the conflict is between something we've done and who we are in Christ, is to change our behavior. I am a saint who sinned; therefore, I must repent and conform to the truth of who I am in Christ. In this instance, the second form of repentance is involved; a change of mind that results in a change in behavior. Another response would be to justify our behavior by rationalizing it. "I only behaved that way because I was stressed out." Finally, we could justify our behavior by embracing the lie; I behaved that way because that's who I am. I sinned because I am a sinner.

So we ought to see in a very real sense that what we do will either reinforce or severely undermine our identity in Christ. If we consistently act against our identity, then we will conform to our actions and not who we are in Christ. The process of renewing our minds takes time. Likewise, it also takes time to change our behavior. However, the two concepts work in concert with one another. Renewing our mind produces changed behavior, and changed behavior facilitates the process of renewing our minds. So if feel like you can't change your behavior, change your thoughts. If you feel like you can't change your thoughts, change your behavior. Ultimately, we need God's grace to do either and He will freely provide grace and power through the Holy Spirit as we continually seek Him.

Becoming

*"For He made Him who knew no sin to be sin for us, that we might **become** the righteousness of God in Him." (2 Corinthians 5:21 NKJV **emphasis added**)*

God, You are so beautiful! Thank You for who You are, thank You for who I am in You. Lord, help me to become who You have created and called me to be. (my prayer)

NOTE THAT THE extent of this section addresses sanctification, not salvation, which has already been addressed. Although, according to Scripture, an exchange with Jesus that doesn't show any outward evidence in our lives was a false exchange. *"Therefore, brothers, be more diligent to make your calling and election sure." (2 Peter 1:10a WEB)* Apart from a last moment, "death bed" conversion, genuine faith will show forth in outward expression.

Even the thief on the cross showed an outward expression of his newfound faith; *"One of the criminals who was hanged insulted him, saying, 'If you are the Christ, save yourself and us!' But the other answered, and rebuking him said, **'Don't you even fear God, seeing you are under the same condemnation? And we indeed justly, for we receive the due reward for our deeds, but this man has done nothing*** *wrong.'* He said to Jesus, *'Lord, remember me when you come into your Kingdom.'* Jesus said to him, *'Assuredly I tell you, today you will be with me in Paradise.'"* (Luke 23:39-42 WEB **emphasis added**)

Just as it is incumbent upon us to recognize and receive the gift of salvation, we have a responsibility to participate with God in becoming who He calls us to be. *Becoming* is the natural overflow of the presence of God in our lives. When He calls us to something, God always makes the provisions necessary to complete it. *"**His divine power has given us everything we need for life and godliness** through our knowledge of him who called us by his own glory and goodness. Through these **he has given us his very great and precious promises, so that through them you may <u>participate</u> in the divine nature and escape the corruption in the world caused by evil desires.**"* (2 Peter 1:3-4 NIV **emphasis added**)

In a very real sense we are caught between the "already" and "not yet." From here on, I am going to replace 'becoming' with the more biblically applied word 'sanctification.' As we saw earlier in 1 Corinthians 1:2, we have already been sanctified. *"To the church of God in Corinth, to **those sanctified in Christ Jesus** and <u>called to be holy</u>…"* (1 Corinthians 1:2 NIV **emphasis added**) In Hebrews, we find a verse that complements 1 Corinthians 1:2. *"For by one offering **He has perfected forever** those who are <u>being sanctified</u>."* (Hebrews 10:10 NKJV **emphasis added**)

The call of God is a call to holiness. *"As obedient children, do not conform to the evil desires you had when you lived in ignorance. But just as he who called you is holy, so be holy in all you do; for it is written: **'Be holy, because I am holy.'"*** (1 Peter 1:14-16 NIV **emphasis added**) *"**Pursue** peace with all people, and **holiness**, without which no one will see the Lord."* (Hebrews 12:14 NKJV **emphasis added**) This holiness which we are to pursue is obviously something other than the imputed righteousness of Christ that happened when God justified us. It is a practical holiness, a holiness that is lived out and seen in our behavior. This is also evident from 1 Corinthians 1:2 and Hebrews 10:10, quoted above, in which I have underlined the portion of each verse that indicates the call to practical holiness.

Sanctification and holiness have the same meaning. They are synonymous and at their most basic level, they refer to the condition of being set apart, separated, distinct, or different. In the highest sense of the word, it refers to God, Who alone is perfectly Holy (i.e. completely set apart, morally perfect, perfectly just and loving), but He has called us to share in His righteousness, His holiness, and to reflect His glory. With regard to sin, we are called to be sanctified.

From my understanding, there are three levels of sanctification. The first level is known as *positional sanctification* or *justification*, which happens when we are born again. I introduced you to this reality in the last section, **Who I Am**. Positional sanctification is the one-time official act of God by which believers are set apart and have a new identity in Christ. Positional sanctification is synonymous with justification, which is by faith.

The second level is known as *progressive sanctification*. We shouldn't get discouraged or overwhelmed by this, because progressive sanctification is a lifelong journey or process by which we participate with God in becoming who we are in Christ. I need to clarify that by participating with God, I do not mean to imply an equal partnership with God. God has done all the work. Therefore, we participate with God by submitting to Him and walking with Him (cf. Matthew 11:29-30). Since this is where we find ourselves, the here and now, progressive sanctification will be the main focus of this section because *"It is God's will that you should be sanctified." (1 Thessalonians 4:3 NIV)*

121

After a time, the believer ought to notice that a war is taking place within their soul, a civil war of sorts. When we were born again, we were given a new nature that desires to please God. Our old nature has been positionally put to death in Christ, yet it continues to operate as if it were alive and well, reasserting itself, prompting us to continue to sin. Thus, the resulting dilemma is that we find ourselves torn in opposite directions. Our lives are a virtual battleground on which an epic struggle is taking place between two opposing forces. *For the flesh lusts against the Spirit, and the Spirit against the flesh; and these are contrary to one another, so that you do not do the things that you wish.*" (Galatians 5:17 NKJV)

Ironically, while working on this section I read a short story entitled 'Two Wolves' that aptly describes the Christian experience.

TWO WOLVES

"One evening an old Cherokee told his grandson about a battle that goes on inside people. He said, 'My son, the battle is between two wolves inside us all.

One is Evil - It is anger, envy, jealousy, sorrow, regret, greed, arrogance, self-pity, guilt, resentment, inferiority, lies, false pride, superiority, and ego.

The other is Good - It is joy, peace, love, hope, serenity, humility, kindness, benevolence, empathy, generosity, truth, compassion and faith.'

The grandson thought about it for a minute and then asked his grandfather: 'Which wolf wins?'

The old Cherokee simply replied, 'The one you feed.'"

(Author Unknown)

We are all products of our culture and rearing, deeply immersed in the natural world around us. We do not change completely the moment we are born into God's family. But Christians, like infants, are born to grow. To do otherwise would be abnormal. We have been given a new nature by God that we are called to develop, and while we seek to develop the new nature, the old nature will continually reassert itself in our lives. Borrowing an analogy from Dr. Neil Anderson, our souls are like computers. When we were born again, God did not just hit the delete button, erasing from our minds the sinful experiences we had prior to our conversion. Therefore, we have an old program or pattern, that Scripture calls "the flesh." This program is automatic, but we need to overcome it if we are to see victory in our lives. God has given us the means to write over the old program.

We touched upon this verse in **Who I Am.** Nevertheless, the passage in its fullness reinforces the previous paragraph. "*I appeal to you therefore, brothers, by the mercies of God, to present your bodies as a living sacrifice, holy and acceptable to God, which is your spiritual worship. Do not be conformed to this world, but* **be transformed by the renewal of your mind**, *that by testing you may discern what is the will of God, what is good and acceptable and perfect.*" *(Romans 12:1-2 ESV* **emphasis added***)*

Reading and meditating upon the word of God are essential to the process of writing over the old program, or renewing our minds. Recall in **An Assault on Pride by Faith,** where I explained that in the Greek, the word *repent* means to change one's mind or way of thinking. The Bible not only calls us to repentance, to change our minds, it also aides us in repentance, changing our minds.

Jesus prayed; "*Sanctify them in your truth. Your word is truth.*" *(John 17:17 WEB)* The apostle Paul wrote; "*Husbands, love your wives, just as Christ loved the church and gave himself up for her to make her holy, cleansing her by the washing with water through the word, and to present her to himself as a radiant church, without stain or wrinkle or any other blemish, but holy and blameless." (Ephesians 5:25-27 NIV* **emphasis added**)

Reading and meditating on the word of God, while essential to the process of renewing our minds, are not the primary means of sanctification; it is the Holy Spirit Who carries out the work of sanctification in our lives, as we yield to Him. However, this does not diminish the importance of the Word to the process of sanctification, because the Word is not independent of the Spirit. Rather, they work in concert with One another. After all, it is the Spirit Who stirs in us a desire for the Word and enables us to understand it.

"But to us, God revealed them through the Spirit. For the Spirit searches all things, yes, the deep things of God. For who among men knows the things of a man, except the spirit of the man, which is in him? Even so, no one knows the things of God, except God's Spirit. But we received, not the spirit of the world, but the Spirit which is from God, that we might know the things that were freely given to us by God. Which things also we speak, not in words which man's wisdom teaches, but which the Holy Spirit teaches, comparing spiritual things with spiritual things." (1 Corinthians 2:10-13 WEB)

In addition to reading and meditating on the Word, it is important we also must apply it to our lives. As James, the Lord's half-brother (cf. Galatians 1:19), warns in the letter that bears his name; *"But be doers of the word, and not only hearers, deluding your own selves. For if anyone is a hearer of the word and not a doer, he is like a man looking at his natural face in a mirror; for he sees himself, and goes away, and immediately forgets what kind of man he was." (James 1:22-24 WEB)* We must actively seek to cultivate the character traits that the Bible calls us to. *"... make every effort to supplement your faith with virtue, and virtue with knowledge, and knowledge with self-control, and self-control with steadfastness, and steadfastness with godliness, and godliness with brotherly affection, and brotherly affection with love. For if these qualities are yours and are increasing, they keep you from being ineffective or unfruitful in the knowledge of our Lord Jesus Christ."* (2 Peter 1:5-8 ESV) According to Paul, this is the fruit of the Spirit that will manifest itself as we are led by Him. (cf. Galatians 5:22-23)

The Bible uses many active words to call us to the action of becoming. With regard to the computer analogy, the Bible says; *"You were taught, with regard to your former way of life, to* **put off your old self,** *which is being corrupted by its deceitful desires; to be made new in the attitude of your minds; and to* **put on the new self,** *created to be like God in true righteousness and holiness."* (Ephesians 4:22-24 NIV **emphasis added**)

On the real, once again I'm going to take a moment to pull back the curtain on my life. Prayerfully in the past, I've struggled with lust and pornography. When I fall into this sin, I'm operating out of the old self and I've reinforced it by my sin. My fellowship with God becomes strained, because sin causes us to be out of harmony in our relationship with the Father. However, God has not moved, I have. My sin has not affected his ability or desire to fellowship with me.

I can't go on too long in a strained relationship with God, so in keeping with 1 John 1:9, I confess my sin, knowing that He is faithful and just, that He has forgiven me my sins, and has purified me from all unrighteousness. *"If we confess our sins, He is faithful and just to forgive us our sins and to cleanse us from all unrighteousness."* (1 John 1:9 NKJV) For salvation to occur, we must confess or agree with God that we have fallen short of His holy standard. But it must be noted that God's continued forgiveness and cleansing are not dependent upon confession of individual sins. Salvation is dependent upon

125

recognizing one's sinfulness and on faith in Christ alone, by this we have been cleansed and forgiven.

Allow me to take a moment to explain my understanding of 1 John. First John was written to combat a 1st century false teaching known as Gnosticism. So 1 John 1:9 is actually an invitation to become Christian. It was not addressed to or about Orthodox believers. Gnostic heresy had crept into the church and John was confronting it. Gnostics taught that there is a separation between the material and spiritual world. They asserted that matter was evil, but the Spirit was good. In their view, since matter was evil, God could not incarnate in, or take on, a human body. Consequently, they believed that Jesus only came in spirit, and rejected the truth that Jesus came in the flesh.

John immediately dispels this idea in the first sentence of his letter. *"That which was from the beginning, that which we have heard, that which we have seen with our eyes, that which we saw, and our hands touched, concerning the Word of life." (1 John 1:1 WEB)* In John 4:2-3, the apostle makes his opposition to this teaching clear, *"By this you know the Spirit of God: every spirit who confesses that Jesus Christ has come* **in the flesh** *is of God, and every spirit who doesn't confess that Jesus Christ has come* **in the flesh** *is not of God, and this is the spirit of the Antichrist, of whom you have heard that it comes. Now it is in the world already." (WEB* **emphasis added***)*

Furthermore, the Gnostic view caused them to deny the reality of sin because, according to their view, since sin took place in the physical world, it wasn't real or didn't matter. John also confronted this fallacy near the beginning of his letter, *"If we say that we have no sin, we deceive ourselves, and the truth is not in us. 9 If we confess our sins, he is faithful and righteous to forgive us the sins, and to cleanse us from all unrighteousness. ¹⁰If we say that we haven't sinned, we make him a liar, and his word is not in us." (1 John 1:8-10 WEB)*

Notice that verse 9 is couched in between two warnings to those who deny the reality of sin, that is, those who adhered to the Gnostic view. Therefore, we must conclude that John is calling these Gnostics to repent, or change their mind, and come into agreement with God concerning sin.

Finally, we see a shift in chapter 2, where John is clearly addressing believers, *"My dear children." He continues, "I write this to you so that you will not sin. But if anybody does sin, we have one who speaks to the Father in our defense—Jesus Christ, the Righteous One. He is the atoning sacrifice for our sins, and not only for ours but also for the sins of the whole world." (1 John 2:1-2 NIV)* Also, *"I write to you, little children, because your sins are forgiven you for his name's sake." (1 John 2:12 WEB)* Notice that confession is conspicuously absent from these verses. Even though continuous confession isn't necessary to maintain one's salvation or communion with the Lord, it is a vital part of repentance, and repentance, as I emphasized in **An Assault on Pride by Faith**, is a natural part of the Christian life. It is part of the process of sanctification, becoming who we are in Christ, and it helps us maintain fellowship with God.

Yet, regarding my sin of viewing pornography, confession is only the beginning. As implied by the poem, *Two Wolves*, quoted above, I need to starve out and completely forsake the images that I've allowed in my mind, so that I will not live a defeated life. To do this, I renounce the lie that these images could somehow satisfy my sexual nature, loneliness and/or curiosity. Then I come into agreement with the word of God by feeding on it and immersing myself in it. As I engage in the process of renewing my mind, I am reminded *"Let us walk properly, as in the day, not in revelry and drunkenness, not in lewdness and lust, not in strife and envy. But put on the Lord Jesus Christ, and make no provision for the flesh, to fulfill its lusts."* (Romans 13:13-14 NKJV)

The thing about lust and pornography is that it's circular; lust leads to pornography and pornography leads to lust. The more one fills his or her mind with pornographic images, the more their lust is inflamed for more images. *"Flee sexual immorality! 'Every sin that a man does is outside the body,' but he who commits sexual immorality sins against his own body."* (1 Corinthians 6:18 WEB)

It is said that our minds can only hold one conscious thought at a time. Therefore, Scripture memorization is a powerful weapon in the battle against impure thoughts. When I am assaulted with such thoughts, I immediately turn to the Scriptures that I have memorized. *"I have hidden your word in my heart, that I might not sin against you."* (Psalm 119:11 WEB)

One such Scripture passage that has helped me avoid sexually immoral situations is Joseph's response to the advances of Potiphar's wife, found in Genesis 39:6b-12. *"Now Joseph was handsome in form and appearance. And after a time his master's wife cast her eyes on Joseph and said, 'Lie with me.' But he refused and said to his master's wife, 'Behold, because of me my master has no concern about anything in the house, and he has put everything that he has in my charge. He is not greater in this house than I am, nor has he kept back anything from me except you, because you are his wife.* **How then can I do this great wickedness and sin against God?'** *And as she spoke to Joseph day after day, he would not listen to her, to lie beside her or to be with her. But one day, when he went into the house to do his work and none of the men of the house was there in the house, she caught him by his garment, saying, 'Lie with me.'* **But he left his garment in her hand and fled and got out of the house.** *(Genesis 39:6b-12*

ESV **emphasis mine***)* According to this Scripture, knowing it dishonors God, I must flee from sexual sin.

There are some who insist that while the law was ineffective to save, it is efficient for sanctification and though they'd argue otherwise, inevitably this involves work after salvation. But this view is contrary to Scripture. The apostle Paul rebuked the Galatians for falling into this view; *"O foolish Galatians! Who has bewitched you that you should not obey the truth, before whose eyes Jesus Christ was clearly portrayed among you as crucified? This only I want to learn from you: Did you receive the Spirit by the* **works of the law***, or by the hearing of faith? Are you so foolish? Having begun in the Spirit, are you now being made perfect by* **the flesh***?" (Galatians 3:2-3 NKJV* **emphasis added***)* Notice how Paul draws a direct connection between *"works of the law"* and *"the flesh."*

An example of the Christian struggling to become sanctified by the law through the flesh can be found in Romans chapter 7. There is some debate as to whether Paul was referring to something that happened before or after his conversion. Myself, I accept the latter position that this happened after his conversion, because no unsaved man can honestly say *"For I delight in the law of God, in my inner being."* (Verse 22) Or perhaps it wasn't Paul's experience at all, but a position he assumed in order to teach a truth.

"For we know that the law is spiritual, but I am of the flesh, sold under sin. For I do not understand my own actions. For I do not do what I want, but I do the very thing I hate. Now if I do what I do not want, I agree with the law, that it is good. So now it is no longer I who do it, but sin that dwells within me. For I know that nothing good dwells in me, that is, in my flesh. For I have the desire to do what is right, but not the ability to carry it out. For I do not do the good I want, but the evil I do not want is what I keep on doing. Now if I do what I do not want, it is no longer I who do it, but sin that dwells within me. So

I find it to be a law that when I want to do right, evil lies close at hand. For I delight in the law of God, in my inner being, but I see in my members another law waging war against the law of my mind and making me captive to the law of sin that dwells in my members. Wretched man that I am! Who will deliver me from this body of death? Thanks be to God through Jesus Christ our Lord! So then, I myself serve the law of God with my mind, but with my flesh I serve the law of sin." (Romans 7:14-25 ESV)

I identified with this passage during **A Time of Darkness,** but I didn't understand until later that if the passage refers to a post conversion experience, which the context suggests, it isn't about salvation, but sanctification. "All Christians doubtless know something of the state depicted in verses 7:14-25 of chapter 7, but once out of it no one need go through it again."[22] This passage reflects a normal experience for Christians, because we have two natures. Therefore, since we have this ongoing struggle between those opposing natures, we ought to come to the end of ourselves, realizing that the law is insufficient for sanctification.

Even though salvation cannot be attained by obedience to the law, and we are not under the law for sanctification, this does not mean we are lawless. According to Scripture, we are under a new more glorious and superior law. We are under the *"law of the Spirit"* *(Romans 8:2 WEB)*, or the *"law of Christ." (1 Corinthians 9:21 ESV)* Just as the new covenant we are under is more glorious and superior than the old, so the law of the Spirit is more glorious and superior to the old.

"He has made us competent as ministers of a **new covenant**—*not of the letter but of* **the Spirit***; for the letter kills, but* **the Spirit gives life***. Now if the ministry that brought death, which was engraved in letters on stone, came*

with glory, so that the Israelites could not look steadily at the face of Moses because of its glory, fading though it was, will not the **ministry of the Spirit be even more glorious**? If the ministry that condemns men is glorious, how much more glorious is the ministry that brings righteousness! For what was glorious has no glory now in comparison with the **surpassing glory**. And if what was fading away came with glory, how much **greater is the glory** of that which lasts!" (2 Corinthians 3:7-11 NIV **emphasis added**)

"But as it is, Christ has obtained **a ministry that is as much more excellent than the old as the covenant he mediates is better**, since it is enacted on better promises. For if that first covenant had been faultless, there would have been no occasion to look for a second. For he finds fault with them when he says: 'Behold, the days are coming, declares the Lord, when I will establish a **new covenant** with the house of Israel and with the house of Judah, not like the covenant that I made with their fathers on the day when I took them by the hand to bring them out of the land of Egypt. For they did not continue in my covenant, and so I showed no concern for them, declares the Lord. For this is the covenant that I will make with the house of Israel after those days, declares the Lord: **I will put my laws into their minds, and write them on their hearts,** and I will be their God and they shall be my people. And they shall not teach, each one his neighbor and each one his brother, saying, 'Know the Lord,' for they shall all know me, from the least of them to the greatest. For I will be merciful toward their iniquities, and I will remember their sins no more.' In speaking of a **new covenant**, he makes the first one obsolete. And what is becoming obsolete and growing old is ready to vanish away." (Hebrews 8:6-13; Jeremiah 31:31-34' ESV **emphasis added**)

"I will give you a new heart and put a new spirit within you; I will take the heart of stone out of your flesh and give you a heart of flesh. I will put My Spirit

131

within you and cause you to walk in My statutes, and you will keep My judgments and do them." (Ezekiel 36:26-27 NKJV)

(See Appendix B for a brief explanation on Hebrews 8:8-10, and Ezekiel 36:26-27; on how Gentiles have come to share in the New Covenant with Israel.)

Above I emphasized Hebrews 8:10, *"I will put my laws into their minds, and write them on their hearts." (ESV)* Ezekiel 36:26-27 is an excellent parallel passage that clearly refers to the rebirth experience. When we are born again, the Spirit of God immediately takes up residence in us (cf. John 14:17). As God puts His laws in our minds and writes His law on our hearts, our conscience is quickened. However, this quickening may not immediately reveal itself in our lives, as it often takes time for our new conscience to develop. Therefore, it is not uncommon for baby Christians to walk in sin for a time because they haven't become sensitive to the Spirit, or His law, which dwells in them. We become more sensitive to the Spirit by reading and meditating upon the Word of God.

As a newly born Christian, I had an old girlfriend, who sought my advice on aborting her baby. The child was not mine, and I still had hopes that this girl and I would get back to together. So I told her that she should abort. A good while after this incident, my conscience was afflicted. I realized the selfish nature of my advice, and that I was complicit in the murder of an unborn child. I brought the situation before the Lord in prayer, owned my part in the murder, and repented of my sin. Our new conscience is part of the new nature that we are called to develop.

Obviously, there is some carryover of the old covenant law to those now under the new covenant. After all, nine of the Ten

Commandments are reiterated in the New Testament. But the law of the Spirit, dwelling in our hearts, is more penetrating and much more searching than the law engraved on stone could ever be. Sin is much more defined. *"Everyone who sins breaks the law; in fact, sin is lawlessness." (1 John 3:4 NIV)* God's commands are now within us and His word is clear that a fruit of sanctification is obedience to His commands that results in supernatural confidence. *"We know that we have come to know him if we obey his commands." (1 John 2:3 NIV)*

Sanctification, like salvation, is by faith. *"For in the gospel a righteousness from God is revealed,* **a righteousness that is by faith from first to last,** *just as it is written:* **'The righteous will live by faith.'"** *(Romans 1:17 NIV* **emphasis added***)* Therefore *"Let us fix our eyes on Jesus, the author and perfecter of our faith…" (Hebrews 12:2 NIV)* Holiness is produced when we exercise our faith by being completely occupied with the risen Christ. We become who He has called us to be when we are caught up in the beauty of his Person, seeking intimacy with Him. Then the passing pleasures of this world lose their appeal and the things of earth grow strangely dim.

Part of being occupied with Christ is just abiding in Him through prayer. God is crazy in love with you! He aches to connect with you in an intimate way. Imagine a young man who was recently engaged. He is in the military and is now on tour. While away in a foreign land, he has written numerous love letters to his fiancée. She incessantly occupies his thoughts. He pines for her, aches for her with all of his being, desiring just to hear her sweet voice. Similarly, though with more intensity, God's heart aches with holy desire to connect with you. Knowing that we are so deeply loved ought to stir our hearts to spend time with the One who loves us so.

When God awakens us to His call to holiness, we do more become who we are in Christ. In addition to being transformed into

His image, we become aware that this isn't solely about becoming who we are, but we also understand that we are fully engaged in the Great Commission found in Matthew 28:18-20. *"Jesus came to them and spoke to them, saying, 'All authority has been given to me in heaven and on earth. Go, and make disciples of all nations, baptizing them in the name of the Father and of the Son and of the Holy Spirit, teaching them to observe all things that I commanded you. Behold, I am with you always, even to the end of the age.' Amen."* (WEB) God has given us power to influence one another. Changed lives change lives!

In a world where most are eager to fit in, we are called to stand out. *"You are the light of the world. A city located on a hill can't be hidden. Neither do you light a lamp, and put it under a measuring basket, but on a stand; and it shines to all who are in the house. Even so, let your light shine before men; that they may see your good works, and glorify your Father who is in heaven."* (Matthew 5:14-16 WEB) This does not mean that we can't be fashionable, it's our life, rather than appearance, that the world should notice. If our talk and our walk don't agree, our testimony won't amount to much. When nonbelievers see nothing different in our lifestyles, they rightly wonder if our profession of faith is sincere. This is what they see; *"They claim to know God, but by their actions they deny him."* (Titus 1:16 NIV)

We are called to live consistent lives of integrity. *"Live such good lives among the pagans that, though they accuse you of doing wrong, they may see your good deeds and glorify God on the day he visits us."* (1 Peter 2:12 NIV) If you live it, you'll be preaching the Gospel with your life. As one author put it; "Nothing speaks so loudly as the silent eloquence of a holy and consistent life. It is a practical and perpetual sermon!"[23] Holiness has an alluring effect. In a world of plastic people, others will note that you're genuine. This does not negate our responsibility to share our faith verbally, but makes it easier when we do.

134

It should be obvious that there is no room for self-righteous pride in our lives. Holiness without humility is ungodly. We need to always remember that we are not perfect and we ought to be honest with ourselves and others about our struggles. For instance, my weakness is lust, which is fueled by certain images, so I make a conscious effort to avoid these images.

While Scripture clearly calls us to admonish (i.e. gently correct; cf. Romans 15:14, Colossians 3:16) one another, it also warns us not think of ourselves as beyond sins that have dogged us in the past. *"Therefore let him who thinks he stands be careful that he doesn't fall." (1 Corinthians 10:12 WEB)* Nor ought we to look down on a brother or sister who has fallen, rather knowing that we ourselves are prone to fall. Instead, if we are aware that someone is struggling, we ought to encourage them and help them to stand back up.

The apostle Paul is an excellent example of humility. He never forgot who he was before the Lord called him. In fact, he often used his own testimony in the delivery of the Gospel. (cf. Acts 22:3-4; 26:9-11). He also frequently wrote about who he was prior to his conversion in his letters to the churches (cf. 1 Corinthians 15:9; Galatians 1:13-14; Philippians 3:4-6). A prime example of this is found in his first letter to Timothy. *"...I was formerly a blasphemer, a persecutor, and an insolent man. (1 Timothy 1:13 NIV)* As he looked back at who he had been, astonished by the grace of God, he wrote, *"The saying is faithful and worthy of all acceptance, that Christ Jesus came into the world to save sinners; of whom I am chief." (1 Timothy 1:15 WEB)* Paul couldn't get over how the grace of God transformed him from an unbelieving persecutor of the church into a relentless preacher of the Gospel of Jesus Christ.

Sharing about our past failures and being aware of our current struggles, while giving praise to God for His forgiveness and grace, will guard us from having a "holier-than-thou" attitude. Even so, others who do not yet know the Lord may perceive you in such a manner. For this reason, it's necessary to remember that we once were as they are. *"For we ourselves were also once foolish, disobedient, deceived, serving various lusts and pleasures, living in malice and envy, hateful and hating one another." (Titus 3:3 NKJV)*

Those who know you best ought to see the change in your life. *"In regard to these, they think it strange that you do not run with them in the same flood of dissipation, speaking evil of you. They will give an account to Him who is ready to judge the living and the dead." (1 Peter 4:4-5 NKJV)*

Remember, Jesus is divisive. Most will reject the Gospel. Many will reject you for choosing to follow Christ. Strangers will be drawn to you, but when you share with them the hope that is in you, most will initially reject the Gospel. We would do well to remember that it is not us that they are rejecting, but Christ. We must endeavor to pray for our family, friends and strangers to whom we've witnessed. Even if they haven't taken that first step of the spiritual journey in Christ, their life journey is not over yet and God's gift is available for the asking.

Unfortunately, some will not simply be indifferent towards you, but rather they will hate you. (c.f. 1 John 3:13) *"Yes, and all who desire to live godly in Christ Jesus will suffer persecution." (2 Timothy 3:12 WEB)* Jesus warns and encourages us that; *"If the world hates you, you know that it has hated me before it hated you. If you were of the world, the world would love its own. But because you are not of the world, since I chose you out of the world, therefore the world hates you. Remember the word that I said to you: 'A servant is not greater than his lord.' If they persecuted me, they will also persecute you. If they kept my word, they will keep yours also.'" (John 15:18-20 WEB)* I typically pray more fervently for those who have expressed hatred of me, because I know that it's not me they hate, but Christ, Who said,

"Love your enemies and pray for those who persecute you." (Matthew 5:44 ESV)

As of this writing, for those of us living in North America, ridicule and rejection seem to be the worst that can happen for living and sharing our faith. Meanwhile, our brothers and sisters throughout the world undergo banishment, imprisonment, torture, and/or murder for bearing the name of Christ. On the horizon, I foresee that in North America, living and witnessing for Christ will come at a far greater cost than mere ridicule and rejection. The time is coming when quoting certain parts of the Bible will be deemed "hate speech," and sharing the Gospel will be discouraged with fierce intensity.

Getting back to the levels of sanctification, the third and final level is perfect sanctification or *glorification*. Sanctification is completed or perfected in the glorification of the believer, which takes place in heaven. Perfect sanctification is God finishing the work He began in us. *"...being confident of this very thing, that he who began a good work in you will complete it until the day of Jesus Christ. (Philippians 1:6 WEB)* Our destiny as Christians is to become Christ-like; that is, perfect in holiness, in righteousness and purity. *"...predestined to be conformed to the image of his Son..." (Romans 8:29 WEB)* This glorification of the believer will either take place in heaven after death, or at the blessed hope and glorious appearing of Christ; *"Beloved, now we are children of God, and it is not yet revealed what we will be. But we know that, when he is revealed, we will be like him; for we will see him just as he is." (1 John 3:2 WEB)*

Deception

*"But false prophets also arose among the people, as false teachers will also be among you, who will secretly bring in destructive **heresies**, denying even the Master who bought them, bringing on themselves swift destruction." (2 Peter 2:1 WEB **emphasis added**)*

"Beloved, don't believe every spirit, but test the spirits, whether they are of God, because many false prophets have gone out into the world." (1 John 4:1 WEB)

IN THE QUOTE from 2 Peter above, I've highlighted the term heresies. Heresy is essentially a departure from the truth, and it is the foundation of deception. Heresies and deceptions are virtually synonymous. The Bible is filled with warnings about deception. *"But the Spirit says expressly that in later times some will fall away from the faith, paying attention to seducing spirits and doctrines of demons." (1 Timothy 4:1 WEB)* It warns that deception will abound in the last days, leading to a departure from the faith (i.e. apostasy) and that the second coming of Christ will be preceded by a great apostasy. The Scriptures refer to this apostasy as "a falling away." *"Let no man deceive you by any means: for that day shall not come, except there come **a falling away** first, and that man of sin be revealed, the son of perdition." (2 Thessalonians 2:3 NKJV **emphasis added**)*

139

In Acts 20:29-31, Paul reveals his concern for the church to the elders from Ephesus. *"I know that after I leave, savage wolves will come in among you and will not spare the flock. Even from your own number men will arise and distort the truth in order to draw away disciples after them. So be on your guard! Remember that for three years I never stopped warning each of you night and day with tears." (NIV)*

The Lord Jesus reveals events that will occur prior to His return; *"Then many will stumble, and will deliver up one another, and will hate one another. Many false prophets will arise, and will lead many astray." (Matthew 24:10-11 WEB)* I believe that now, more than in previous generations, we are susceptible to deception and apostasy. This is in large part because most of us lack spiritual discernment (i.e. proper judgment). Oddly, the Bible is more readily available today than in centuries past, and in North America we have a literacy rate of 99%. Despite this, the Bible has become less prominent today, as it seems society has more interest in popular culture than in the Bible. We, as a society, don't take the Bible seriously anymore; therefore, we are inadvertently fulfilling Bible prophecy as we quickly approach the point of no return.

It is my prayer that my writing encourages you to read and study the Word of God for yourself. I don't want you to take my word regarding things of the Bible. I hope to inspire you to read and examine these things on your own. I want you to be a Berean! *"Now the Bereans were of more noble character than the Thessalonians, for they received the message with great eagerness and examined the Scriptures every day to see if what Paul said was true." (Acts 17:11 NIV)*

Even with a 99% literacy rate and the availability of the Bible, most Christians are content to be spoon-fed the Word of God. Consequently, they are unable to discern when the Bible is being mishandled or manipulated. The Bible warns that in the last days, many churchgoers in fact will have no desire to hear the Word of God preached, or they will want it changed to suit their desires. *"For the time is coming when people will not endure sound teaching, but having itching ears they will accumulate for themselves teachers to suit their own passions." (2 Timothy 4:3 ESV)*

Contrary to popular belief, the Bible isn't difficult to read or understand, especially once you've been born again. However, I must warn you against getting hung up on the correct pronunciation of the names of people and places. This happened to my sister Laurie, who read the four gospels, but when she came to The Acts of the Apostles, also known as Acts, she allowed herself to be overwhelmed by the names of people and places. My advice is to just take note of the name, pronouncing it to the best of your ability, and then move along. Even if there are words you don't immediately understand, don't stress out or allow this to discourage you. This is part of the learning process.

When I was new to the faith, I almost fell into deception. Without much prayerful guidance, I fell under the influence of the heretical teaching of the *Philadelphia Church of God* (PCG). Since being saved, I've always had an interest in Bible prophecy, because it was one of the main elements that convinced me of the credibility of the Bible. "The fulfillment of prophecy provides tangible, empirical evidence which proves beyond any doubt that the Bible is inspired of God and that we can count upon all that it says."[24] Satan, seeing an opportunity to take advantage of my interest, took aim to deceive me. He has deceived many, using false prophets and teachers as his instruments.

I came across a program called *The Key of David,* while watching a secular station on which had other Bible preachers and teachers I enjoyed. On this program they offered free pamphlets on "Bible" prophecy. I read countless pamphlets, and was in the midst of a book by their teacher, Herbert W. Armstrong, before being jarred awake by a death.

Armstrong, who passed away in 1986, proclaimed himself to be an "Apostle," and many of his followers herald him as an end time prophet, in the mold of Elijah or John the Baptist. He proclaimed that his writings were divinely inspired. The PCG still hold tightly to his teachings, which on their face are absurdly non-biblical, but I was captured by his writing style, being blind to the many nuances that when placed together, reveal a significant departure from biblical Christianity.

Like a 20th century Joseph Smith (the founder of the Church of Jesus Christ of Latter Day Saints, also known as LDS or Mormonism), Armstrong asserted that modern Christianity was not based on the Bible, but on a distorted and twisted interpretation of the Bible. He claimed that God restored the truth through his teaching.

It would be futile to enumerate the false teachings of the PCG, which were very legalistic. I just want you to understand where I was at spiritually before the next event took place. I also want you to be aware that there are cults out there and that deception abounds. The best way to recognize a cult (i.e. a counterfeit) is to know the real thing. On the United States Secret Service website, it says this regarding how to detect counterfeit money, "Look at the money you receive. Compare a suspect note with a genuine note of the same denomination and series, paying attention to the quality of printing and paper characteristics. Look for differences, not similarities." [25] This is the optimal way to identify a cult as well. Know the Bible and compare every teaching to Scripture.

Many modern day prophets, while their "prophecies" tend to divert away from the Bible and contradict biblical revelation, still claim to represent the God of the Bible. Many insist that their revelation supersedes what God has revealed in the Bible. But this cannot be, because biblical Scripture clearly teaches that God is unchangeable. *"For I the LORD do not change." (Malachi 3:6 ESV)* Also Hebrews 6:17-18 states, *"So when God desired to show more convincingly to the heirs of the promise the unchangeable character of his purpose, he guaranteed it with an oath, so that by two unchangeable things, in which it is impossible for God to lie, we who have fled for refuge might have strong encouragement to hold fast to the hope set before us." (ESV)* Therefore, if God gives us a personal word, or should He choose to give new revelation, it must be consistent with His original revelation found in the Bible. As Paul warned, *"Do not go beyond what is written." (1 Corinthians 4:6 NIV)*

Many false prophets and teachers are date setters. They think they are privy to some special knowledge or technique, which enables them to determine when Christ will return. They ignore the clear teaching of Jesus concerning His second coming; *"But concerning that day and hour no one knows, not even the angels of heaven, nor the Son, but the Father only." (Matthew 24:36 ESV)*

The apostle Paul was concerned about the influence of false gospels. He wrote; *"I am astonished that you are so quickly deserting him who called you in the grace of Christ and are turning to a different gospel—not that there is another one, but there are some who trouble you and want to distort the gospel of Christ. But even if we or an angel from heaven should preach to you a gospel contrary to the one we preached to you, let him be accursed. As we have said before, so now I say again: If anyone is preaching to you a gospel contrary to the one you received, let him be accursed." (Galatians 1:6-9 ESV)*

143

A Young Death

"…it is appointed for man to die once." (Hebrews 9:27 ESV)

THE SUNDAY MORNING of July 2nd 2000, my mom came into my room crying. She had received some terrible news. Brea had been killed in a motorcycle accident.

She was at a party on Saturday July 1st, and a young man who had just bought a crotch rocket offered to take her for a ride. Apparently, the young man was a novice with a new motorcycle, and with Brea on the back, he supposedly clipped the back of a car, throwing them into the other lane, into oncoming traffic. Alcohol was not a factor.

I don't know how people, like my mom, can absorb the reality of death so quickly. It was surreal to me, so I acted like I thought one should act – distraught. I wrote this poem for her, myself, her family and others who were struggling to understand why. It reveals my shallow understanding of the Bible at the time, but also a reverential trust in God. It was read at her funeral.

O' God

O' God why o' why must young people die

I can't see any good that comes from death

All that I can see is pain and heartache

We weep and mourn all day

At night we toss and turn

Wondering if there was something we could have done

But all that's left is to trust in your only Son

We ask how You could let this happen

But we get no answer, only silence

And many of us turn our backs on You

But maybe this is a test to see who will stay true to You

But after all our questions are asked

We come to this hard fact

That man can never understand

Your one true holy plan

I don't know why I wrote it for young people in general, rather than just for Brea. But I would soon turn to this question of "why" again, and perhaps that's the reason why I wrote the way I did.

Still, no tears at the funeral. The casket was closed with her recent graduation picture on top. It wasn't until several days later that my emotions finally caught up with reality. The tears flowed freely, I was finally mourning.

It's kind of hard to describe the way I felt; hurt, confused, angry, and just crushed. I was grasping for answers that would never come. It wasn't that I was simply angry with God. My emotions towards God were more complex than mere anger. I was overwhelmed with a mixture of disappointment and confusion as well.

During this time I wrote several poems for Brea, to give me an emotional release as I struggled with regret for what might have been. Here's a sampling;

Sorry

My love is gone away
And I'm so sad because I didn't tell her how sorry I was
Now I'm sorry every single day
I'm filled with so much sorrow
Because I always had to wait until tomorrow
I never got to tell her how much I love her
And now I never will
I was always a procrastinator
Things could always wait until later
But never again
Because it feels like a sin
Never again will I wait
To tell somebody how much I care about them

Hearts Breaking

Every time I think of you
My heart begins to break in two
I didn't know how much I cared about you until you were gone
Now I think about you all night long
Who would have ever thought you'd die before me
I feel like I don't even deserve to be

You comforted me when my time had almost come
Now I miss you so much my body feels numb
I was there, the heavens cried when you died
Now I talk to the air but I don't care
It's just not the same
I feel so ashamed
Because I didn't tell you how I felt before
How much I love you

As I stated earlier, I was now fully aware of what I was reading in regards to the PCG. I found no comfort in their writings. In fact, I was distressed because according to their literature you had to be a member of their church in order to *obtain* salvation. Any time a specific church, denomination or organization claims to be the only way to salvation, it's a pretty good indication that they are a cult. Jesus said, *"I am the way, and the truth, and the life. No one comes to the Father except through me." (John 14:6 ESV)* And Peter proclaimed, *"Salvation is found in no one else, for there is no other name under heaven given to men by which we must be saved." (Acts 4:12 NIV)* Salvation is found in the person of Christ alone, not in a certain religious organization, denomination or church.

So with little difficulty I discarded all of the PCG material I had, and rededicated myself to familiarizing myself with the genuine Gospel. Though much had happened that was beyond my understanding, I wasn't going to abandon this new found faith that had brought more peace and joy than I had ever known. So I pressed in deeper!

Self-Forgiveness and Acceptance

There is therefore now no condemnation for those who are in Christ Jesus.
(Romans 8:1 ESV)

ON OCCASION, WE would go to church where my mom's cousin, Tom, attended. It was called Immanuel, and it was located in Roseville, Michigan, about a 45-minute drive south of Port Huron. At the church, they were laying hands on people and praying for them.

Tom stepped to me and said, "You haven't forgiven yourself for the accident, have you Ryan." Something inside me broke as I said "no" and started crying, balling really. Sometimes the hardest grudges to let go of are the ones we hold against ourselves.

Tom led me in a liberating prayer of self-forgiveness. I stopped fighting God and myself, and came to a place of acceptance; acceptance of self and of the affliction. Though I suspect I knew all along, I was now in a position where I was able to understand what God was doing with me. I take a different point of view than most. I don't believe that the crash was "part of God's plan." Such thinking is fatalistic and discourages individual responsibility. While it is true that God, being eternal and outside of time, already knows the decisions we will make, this does not negate the reality of our decisions. They are still ours; they are not mere illusions.

149

That is not to say that our decisions are not influenced by unseen forces, both good and evil. They are. For example, even though from God's eternal perspective it had already occurred, from my perspective, if I had heeded the warnings that I referred to in **Being Drawn,** the crash would have been avoided. The crash happened as a result of a series of bad decisions, the worst being my choice to ignore God. I believe that God redeemed the crash, using it to get my attention.

"God whispers to us in our pleasures, speaks in our conscience, but shouts in our pain; it is His megaphone to rouse a deaf world."[26]

But those who suffer he delivers in their suffering; he speaks to them in their affliction. (Job 36:15 NIV)

Well, God definitely had my attention. He was speaking to me in and through my affliction, and I was listening. I identified with Psalm 119:65-72, which reads;

You have dealt well with your servant,
O Lord, according to your word.
Teach me good judgment and knowledge,
for I believe in your commandments.
Before I was afflicted I went astray,
but now I keep your word.
You are good and do good;
teach me your statutes.
The insolent smear me with lies,
but with my whole heart I keep your precepts;
their heart is unfeeling like fat,

but I delight in your law.
It is good for me that I was afflicted,
that I might learn your statutes.
The law of your mouth is better to me
than thousands of gold and silver pieces. (NKJV **emphasis added***)*

I was beginning to see what God was doing in me. I was changing from the inside out. I was growing spiritually. *"Behold, I have refined you, but not as silver; I have tried you in the furnace of affliction." (Isaiah 48:10 ESV)*

War

"For our struggle is not against flesh and blood, but against the rulers, against the authorities, against the powers of this dark world and against the spiritual forces of evil in the heavenly realms." (Ephesians 6:12 NIV)

"There is something in human nature that just doesn't want to face the reality that we live in two worlds. We live in the physical, material world where we have jobs, read books, and go about our business. And we live in a spiritual world – and that is a world at war." (John Eldridge)[27]

BEFORE I WAS born again, I had always acknowledged what the Bible said about Satan and his demonic minions as being true. It is apparent that evil is a part of this world and biblical Christianity's explanation of the fall of man is the only one that confronts the reality of evil head on. There is a quote from the movie *The Usual Suspects* that always stuck with me; "The greatest trick the Devil ever pulled was convincing the world he didn't exist."[28] I'd like to amend this quote from "didn't" to doesn't, for the trick is ongoing. The devil still exists, as I would soon find out.

Sometime after my rebirth experience, I became more aware of another reality. I don't remember if it was a gradual thing or if it happened all at once, but it sure felt like the latter. My mind was under assault, as my thoughts were bent upon complete evil. Most evil has a certain glamour to it and comes in the form of temptation. Well, there was no glamour in these; I can't even describe the thoughts. Though I knew it wasn't me, I was ashamed that such thoughts were in my mind. I hated the thoughts. With them came condemning thoughts that caused me to question my conversion and salvation. It didn't take me long to come to the conclusion that since I was opposed to these thoughts, their source must be other than me. Was I going crazy? Had my mind become the devil's playground?

I had determined that the source of the thoughts was demonic, but this knowledge did little, other than frighten me. Was I possessed? Was I evil? Had God rejected me? I did not know how to battle this enemy, I felt alone and afraid. Who would or could understand this?

I had my dad drive me up to the local Family Christian Bookstore, where I bluntly stated that I was suffering under demonic attacks, and asked if they had any books on spiritual warfare. I can still remember the desperation in my voice. The woman working just calmly handed me a book by Dr. Neil Anderson called, *The Bondage Breaker*. I highly recommend this book to every believer, whether or not you are actively experiencing spiritual conflict. It is essential to the Christian walk to understand spiritual conflict and its root causes, as everyone struggles with demons.

"Submit yourselves therefore to God. Resist the devil, and he will flee from you." (James 4:7 ESV) Anderson writes that in order to resist the devil, it is imperative that we first understand and appropriate our identity, position and authority in Christ. Not only is this imperative

for spiritual warfare, it is also an essential element of confidence for the believer.

Christ testified of the Devil that *"he is a liar and the father of lies."* *(John 8:44 NIV)* When we sin, we come into agreement with a lie, and surrender ground to the Enemy. As a result, we give Satan a place in our lives and souls. Jesus also declared that *"the truth will set you free."* *(John 8:32 ESV)* Therein we see the battle lines; lies, which lead to sin and bondage, or the truth, which sets us free.

In order to reclaim what we have surrendered, we must utilize the gift of repentance, through Jesus Christ. That is, taking responsibility for sin, even if it was one of your ancestors (cf. Numbers 14:18), and coming into agreement with God by declaring the truth and turning away from sin. In this instance, repentance is a change of mind that results in a change of direction. It is our individual responsibility as believers to repent and believe the truth that will set us free. For repentance to be effective in spiritual warfare, it must be done aloud. The Enemy is not all knowing, he cannot read our minds. When we repent aloud, declare the truth and renounce the lie with which we once agreed, we put Satan on notice and since he has been defeated, he must relinquish territory. *"For though we live in the world, we do not wage war as the world does. The weapons we fight with are not the weapons of the world. On the contrary, they have divine power to demolish* **strongholds.** *We demolish arguments and every pretension that sets itself up against the knowledge of God, and we take captive every thought to make it obedient to Christ." (2 Corinthians 10:3-5 NIV* **emphasis added)**

The Bondage Breaker led me through a process of repentance, called the *Steps to Freedom in Christ.* Initially, after completing the steps, I felt genuine relief, though it took a good week for everything to get worked out in the spiritual realm.

Knowing the Enemy

"There are two equal and opposite errors into which our race can fall about the devils. One is to disbelieve in their existence. The other is to believe, and to feel an excessive and unhealthy interest in them."[29] (C.S. Lewis; The Screwtape Letters)

I'D LIKE TO take some space to expose a lie the devil has most of the western world under. It is similar to "the greatest trick," and it is just as sinister. This lie recognizes the existence of the devil, but characterizes him as some innocuous red creature with hoofed feet, horns, a tail and a pitchfork. Who would take such a character seriously? It's the stuff of cartoons! I don't want to dwell on him too long, but it is imperative that we know our enemy, in order to be properly aware of his schemes.

The picture the Bible paints of the devil is much different from our red-horned menace;

*"Son of man, take up a lamentation for the king of Tyre, and say to him, 'Thus says the Lord GOD: You were the seal of perfection, full of wisdom and perfect in beauty. You were in Eden, the garden of God; every precious stone was your covering: the sardius, topaz, and diamond, beryl, onyx, and jasper, sapphire, turquoise, and emerald with gold. The workmanship of your timbrels and pipes was prepared for you on the day you were **created**. You were the anointed*

cherub who covers; I established you; you were on the holy mountain of God; you walked back and forth in the midst of fiery stones. You were perfect in your ways from the day you were created, till iniquity was found in you. By the abundance of your trading you became filled with violence within, and you sinned; therefore I cast you as a profane thing out of the mountain of God; and I destroyed you, O covering cherub, from the midst of the fiery stones. Your heart was lifted up because of your beauty; you corrupted your wisdom for the sake of your splendor; I cast you to the ground, I laid you before kings that they might gaze at you. You defiled your sanctuaries by the multitude of your iniquities, by the iniquity of your trading; therefore I brought fire from your midst; it devoured you, and I turned you to ashes upon the earth in the sight of all who saw you."' (Ezekiel 28:12-18 NKJV **emphasis added***)*

Obviously, this passage of Scripture isn't speaking of a mere man. I highlighted **created** above, just to point out that men are born, angels were created. That is to say, human beings are procreated, in the womb of a woman, while angels were created directly by God.

I think it goes beyond our imaginations, being tainted by sin, to rightly imagine such a creature as beautiful and perfect as this anointed guardian cherub (i.e. angel) was. Nevertheless, this is a picture of Satan before he fell from heaven, and as we see from the above passage, he became proud because of his beauty. The following passage from Isaiah completes the picture of the result of Satan's pride.

"How you are fallen from heaven, O Lucifer, son of the morning! How you are cut down to the ground, you who weakened the nations! For you have said in your heart: 'I will ascend into heaven, I will exalt my throne above the stars of God; I will also sit on the mount of the congregation on the farthest sides of the

north; I will ascend above the heights of the clouds, I will be like the Most High.'
Yet you shall be brought down to Sheol, To the lowest depths of the Pit." (Isaiah
14:12-15 NKJV)

The word *Lucifer* is the Latin translation of a Hebrew term that means *light-bearer*. Before his fall, light-bearer described the devil's standing before God. After his fall from heaven, God gave Lucifer a new name, *Satan*. Satan means *adversary* and therefore describes the devil's current standing before God.

Getting back to the passage quoted above, admittedly the context of this passage, like the one from Ezekiel, is addressed to a king, the king of Babylon. But there is general consensus within Christendom that these passages refer to a spiritual force beyond the earthly kings. This is likely due to the fact that they confer with the rest of what Scripture reveals about Satan. Let's look at Luke 10:18, 1 Timothy 3:6 and Revelation 12:7-9.

"I saw Satan fall like lightning from heaven." (Luke 10:18 NIV)

The context in the following verse refers to the requirements for the office of bishop. *"…not a novice, lest being puffed up with pride he fall into the same condemnation as the devil." (1 Timothy 3:6 NKJV)*

"Now war arose in heaven, Michael and his angels fighting against the dragon. And the dragon and his angels fought back, but he was defeated, and there was no longer any place for them in heaven. And the great dragon was thrown down, that ancient serpent, who is called the devil and Satan, the deceiver of the whole world—he was thrown down to the earth, and his angels were thrown down with him." (Revelation 12:7-9 ESV)

Even though the above verse from Revelation depicts the Enemy as a dragon, this refers more to his character than his appearance. *"And no wonder, for even Satan masquerades as an angel of light." (2 Corinthians 11:14 WEB)* While this clearly states that he is no longer an angel of light, there is no scriptural indication that Satan lost his beauty. Nor does Scripture indicate that he retained his beauty. The Bible often uses light and darkness as metaphors for good and evil. Therefore, though he is shrouded in darkness or pure evil, there is evidence that leads me to believe that the devil retained his beauty. The evidence is sin. We are caught by sin when we are tempted; sin is attractive to our fallen nature, hence temptation. Since sin is attractive, it stands to reason that its source is as well, at least superficially. Sin is deceitful, holding the illusion of gratification, but leading to bondage and ultimately, destruction. *"The thief only comes to steal, kill, and destroy..." (John 10:10 WEB)*

By the way, 2 Corinthians 11:15 completes the thought of 2 Corinthians 11:14 quoted above, *"And no wonder, for Satan himself masquerades as an angel of light. It is not surprising, then, if his servants masquerade as servants of righteousness." (2 Corinthians 11:14-15 NIV)* This confirms that light and darkness are often used metaphorically. It also reveals that Satan can change our perception of his character.

Of course God could have destroyed Satan the moment he rebelled; but this apparently would not have proven that God is holy, only that He is all powerful. The destruction of Satan is not in line with God's holy character. If it were, then God would actually be the cosmic tyrant some accuse Him of being. I contend that our sense of evil requires the holy God of the Bible; a God who is perfect, just and good. Otherwise, our moral indignation at evil would be complete nonsense. God battles evil, and will conquer it.

Or rather, as we have seen, God has battled evil and has conquered it. However, He has not yet implemented the victory in its fullness.

Not Alone

APPROXIMATELY TWO AND a half years after the accident, I was contacted via e-mail by a friend of mine who was recently released from prison. I was concerned about him, and warned him about the power of influence. I told him that if he wanted to stay out of prison, he should not hang out with the same people as before. I mentioned several relationships that I knew were bad influences, because I was part of that crowd and consequently, I was a bad influence as well.

Among the names that I had mentioned in the email was Geoff Harris. On March 4th 2001, I received an e-mail from Geoff's little sister, Crystal. She informed me that Geoff was not a bad influence, that he was no longer able to influence anybody since he had died in the crash. Geoff was my passenger that night, his neck was broken upon impact and he had died instantly.

I cried out, "Oh my God!" My mom heard me and came running to my room to see what was wrong. I showed her the e-mail and asked her if it was so. With tears in her eyes, she confirmed that yes, Geoff had been with me that night and was killed in the crash. She explained that the psychologists told them to keep this from me because such knowledge would only hinder my rehabilitation. I understood that my parents loved me and they thought that keeping this from me was the best thing for me. Being one that tends to internalize things, they were likely right. I probably would have lost all motivation or surrendered to the suicidal thoughts that had plagued me.

As I wrote earlier with regards to Brea, death always seems surreal to me at first. I had always felt guilty for my immediate lack of response to tragedy. But after earning a Bachelor's degree in psychology, I recognized this as a common part of the grieving process, called denial. As the reality of Geoff's death began to settle in, I felt robbed of the natural mourning process which comes with the death of a loved one. Most had already mourned and were moving on with life, while I was just then being caught up and coming to grips with reality. An example of God's supernatural timing – after a 3-month hiatus, I was scheduled to see my counselor, Dave, the next day.

I obviously still had no memory of the crash, but with everything out in the open now, my parents were able to fill in some of the gaps. Apparently, Geoff had recently turned 17 and had borrowed another friend's ID to go to Canada with me and a group of our friends to celebrate his birthday. Geoff was a big kid and could have easily passed for someone in his early twenties.

The evening of the crash, my parents were contacted by the Canadian authorities and told that they needed to come to Sarnia, that there had been a fatality. My sister Laurie, who actually received the call, beat my parents to the hospital. When they saw her out front emotionally arguing with a priest, they were afraid to get out of the vehicle, for fear that I had died. The authorities must have found out that Geoff borrowed someone else's identification, probably by calling the parents of the man to whom the ID belonged. My parents had never met Geoff, so they were tasked with trying to find out who his parents were, in order to notify them of the crash. They retrieved a list of phone numbers for most of my friends that I had at that time. When they came to Geoff's number, his mom answered and said that her son was with Ryan Krafft last night, and that he hadn't come home.

I learned, as I touched upon earlier, that after partying in Canada we headed home after 2 AM. When turning left at an intersection, traveling approximately 15 mph, we were broadsided or t-boned by a 1-ton pickup truck going approximately 65 mph, in a 30 mph zone. The driver of the other vehicle had been drinking as well, but he knew the police officers who had arrived at the scene. So, coincidentally, they didn't have a breathalyzer test available. This was all in the police report. Afterward, when my dad questioned this, he was told that administering a breathalyzer was at the field officer's discretion. The question then became who ran the red light. With no eyewitnesses, it was ruled 50/50 fault.

However, somehow they had me up on manslaughter charges. It took letters of appeal from Geoff's mom and sister to the Crown Attorney before the charges were formally dropped. Why the Crown was so intent on prosecuting me while letting the other driver off scot free, I don't know. All of this played out while I was in a coma.

In the back of my mind, I think I always knew somebody was with me. But I wanted so badly for it to just be me in the crash that I had convinced myself that it was. I had many friends from numerous cliques that were never there for me. They never called or visited. So I had just assumed that Geoff was one of these.

Geoff and I had worked together at Buff's Carwash. We quickly became buddies. More than that, we were kindred spirits. He was always such a joy to be around, joking and laughing. In the end

165

though, the thing that bound us together, the love of the party, would be our undoing; killing him and leaving me crippled.

Even though I realized that God was preparing me for this through trials, like the Deception, Brea's death, Self-Forgiveness, the War, and A Time of Darkness, I still felt betrayed by God and put a lot of blame on myself. I was genuinely angry with God. I felt like I thought I had known Him, but this changed things. I wrestled with God for several days. When I finally got quiet enough to listen and think clearly, I felt God remind me "I am the same yesterday, today and forever." This comes from Hebrews 13:8 *"Jesus Christ is the same yesterday, today, and forever." (WEB)*

It wasn't hard for me to discern what God was trying to get across. He had not changed. Even when God was drawing me after the crash, Geoff's death had always been a reality. I just didn't know about it. God had not changed; He was still God. Rather it was my perception of Him based on a previously unknown reality that had changed. Once I came to terms with God, it was easier to forgive myself.

Back to Life

ON November 4th 2000, my niece Kylee was born to Nikki and PJ. I have been blessed with the opportunity to watch my nieces and nephews grow, mature, and to be a part of their lives. Laurie and Steve had Colby and Chelsea, while Nikki and PJ had Travis, Chase and Kylee.

Most of what follows, being written from memory, will lack the dynamic life of the 4/19/12 incident, still to come in the book, in which I wrote in story format the day after, with the intent of sharing it with others. It opened my eyes to the writing that I'm capable of and how woefully short this endeavor falls of that. Perhaps journals ought to be written with the intent that others read them. I am now attempting to journal consistently with this thought in mind. Most of the following events will not have any specific dates, some will break free of the chronological order in which they occurred; parts will just be a summary of an entire area of experience. For that reason, I've chosen to break up this section, and its follow-up, **Back to Life Again,** into subsections. (e.g. Music, Friends)

Home Improvement

For a while after the crash, my parents and I thought about moving and explored places to move in order to build or refurbish a house, since ours was obviously not handicap friendly. We couldn't agree on anything, except that we liked our house and the neighborhood where we lived. So we hired my brother-in-law Steve to put an addition on the house. Whatever I write is going to fall short of the awesome job that Steve did. If you don't know Steve, he's a perfectionist, attentive to every detail.

My parents gave up their master bedroom and Steve added on to the front of the house, off their room. He transformed their bathroom, no…transformed isn't the right word. He used the existing plumbing to create an entirely new bathroom with a roll-in shower and Jacuzzi tub. He made an enlarged hallway from the front door into the room. He did some work on my bedroom to make it a little bigger. I was moved into the master bedroom with the new addition and new bathroom, while my parents moved into my room. They have ceaselessly sacrificed their own comfort to do what they could to make my life easier.

Therapy/Back to the Gym

Eventually the insurance company stopped paying for therapy. Before the crash, I exercised at the Port Huron Fitness Center, and before my physical therapist Sue moved on, she helped me back into a routine, as well as aquatic therapy in the pool. My dad always assisted with my physical therapy, so when Sue was done he picked up where she left off. I had hit a plateau in my recovery. I was just maintaining what I had worked so hard to get back. After a while, my sister Laurie quit her job, so that she could help my dad with me.

I want to take a moment to honor my parents. While my dad can be grouchy and at times altogether irritable, this man literally gave himself completely to the task of seeing me recover as much as possible. When most fathers would have up and left, he came by my side and carried my cross with me, helping me shoulder the weight. Over time we became more than father and son. We became best friends. My mom is a beautiful woman inside and out. She retired in 2003. She had broken her right wrist in a fall on the ice in 1997, and as a result she had a titanium plate surgically implanted, in order to set it. Therefore, she is limited in helping me with a lot of physical activity. But her presence is indispensable. She keeps the household going, and of course being my mother, she mothers me.

Friends

My dad becoming my best friend likely happened because after a while my friends stopped coming around completely. No more drop in visits. I seldom ever even received a phone call. And when I did, the friend on the other end would make plans to come see me, but most of the time, when the time would come, I would get excited and wait, only to be let down because they'd never come. I wish it was, but this was not an isolated event. It happened on numerous occasions. I couldn't figure it out. I wasn't the drooling mess I once was, I could hold my head up and even speak. I felt totally abandoned. I grew cynical and hardhearted, but to this day, I still give people the benefit of the doubt. I just learned not to get my hopes up.

On a few occasions, I would see a friend at the mall, and they'd act like they didn't see me and/or go off in a different direction. I felt that I could identify with the psalmist; *"My friends and companions avoid me because of my wounds; my neighbors stay far away." (Psalm 38:11*

169

NIV) All this happened before I had any real faith. But it freed me up to go all in for Jesus. In hindsight, I believe that God allowed relationships that were not healthy for me to be severed, so that I'd be more prepared for a relationship with Him.

Several years later, certain friends who knew of my faith would return, but only for a short time. Their inevitable departure always hurt. In 2007, as the tired pain of seeing another come and go was at its peak, I wrote this poem;

Abandoned...again

The pain of the last has hardly dulled
Before another one comes and goes/
They all fall away
Seems no one's ever here to stay/
I just wanna be real
Want to show you how I feel/
I don't hate you/ I'm not like you
I don't want you to feel like I do/
Why can't you just be real?
Why with your lies must I always deal?/
I didn't recognize
I could almost see the lies in your eyes/
You left a scar in my heart
You're all tearing me apart/
I hide my disgust
It's not becoming – so I must/
I hate that you treat me this way
You justify – and think it's okay/
Because what can I do?

I'm not the type to unleash the anger inside
Even beneath these words – its fullness hides/
So I build them higher
These walls of insecurity/
A dam – they've become
Holding back the anger and the pain
Somehow I've become the one you disdain/
Why do I let it bother me?
And you can't even see what you're doing!!!

It seems pretty dramatic now, but I still remember how intense the sense of abandonment and loneliness felt. Earlier, I wrote how I assumed that Geoff hadn't abandoned me, but was one of those many friends who was never there for me. Sounds confusing, but what I mean is that I only truly felt abandoned by those who were there for a time after the crash, while those who were never there, though I'm sure they had their reasons, I disregarded entirely. Well, now Geoff has a place in my life and heart that is very unique. He will always be a part of me.

Music

My CD collection of 100 plus discs was lost or stolen from my truck during the aftermath of the crash. When I found out, I immediately began an effort to rebuild my collection with new CDs. Before I was out of the hospital, I asked my sister Nicole to buy me some Pantera for my birthday. I also bought music by KoRn, Limp Biscuit, Three Six Mafia, The Dayton Boyz, Eninem and the like.

I wish that I was able to share that immediately after I was born again my music habits changed. But it took time. I respected my nurse aide, Tresa, enough not to play my music around her, basically

171

confirming that I knew it was trash. Many claim that they can listen to music and be unaffected by the lyrical content. How anybody can play in the garbage and not come out stinking is beyond me. I certainly couldn't. I recounted at the end of **Who I Was** the powerful influence music had on me. It influenced my thoughts, my talk and my walk.

I think that the general perception outside of Christendom is that Christian musicians lack talent. I've found that the exact opposite is true. Tresa introduced me to Christian contemporary music, which was good, but a far cry from the genres I liked. Somehow I stumbled across a band named Justifide. They were a rap core/nu metal band that was right up my alley.

In 2002, I was able to see them in concert on the All The Way Live tour. The headline band was Thousand Foot Krutch, whom I'd actually never heard of up until then. In 2006, Justifide disbanded, changed names, style, and lost an edge. But that night, Thousand Foot Krutch (TFK) lit it up and I've been a big fan of theirs since.

I could go on and on about the bands I now like as well as the many concerts I've been fortunate enough to attend. But the point is that my musical entertainment was an area that I needed to surrender to the Lord. This was my first conscious step of obedience and it was a life changer.

Back to School and 9/11

In the fall of 2001, I returned to my studies at St. Clair Community College, with an initial interest in psychology, due to Dave's influence. Another factor that played into my decision to shift away from mechanical engineering is that my passion changed. Before the crash, I enjoyed math and I was good at it. Now, it seemed that I had lost most of my math skills and the passion along with it. I had taken Psychology 101 before the crash because it was a prerequisite. I only took one course upon my reentry; Abnormal Psychology.

Writing about the fall of 2001 brings to mind the terror attack on 9/11. I turned on CNN to hear about the first plane striking the tower and listened to the commentators try to rationalize how a plane could run into the World Trade Center's North Tower. It seemed to never occur to them that it might be intentional. It was 9:00 am, so I flipped to CBN and they immediately called it what it was, a terrorist attack. Shortly thereafter, at 9:03, somebody was talking to my mom on the phone and told her that a 2nd plane had hit the other tower. So I flipped back to CNN, because they had a live feed. I remember it seemed like forever until CNN made any reference to foul play. It was all so surreal, like watching a movie.

I was glued to the coverage, but I had class at 10:00 that morning, so at 9:30 my sister Laurie and I left for school. It wasn't until after class that I learned that American Airlines Flight 11 had been crashed into the North Tower; followed by United Airlines Flight 175 crashing into the South Tower. American Airlines Flight 77 had hit the Pentagon. We were watching the aftermath of United Airlines Flight 93, which was forced down in a field in Pennsylvania. We were at war!

False rumors were being circulated that a plane in Michigan had been hijacked and was flying somewhere over Detroit. Before we left for home, Laurie and I went to the library to catch up on the coverage. Honestly, the only emotions I felt on 9/11 were awe and denial that gave way to anger. It felt as if we'd been raped! I didn't shed a tear for the victims until a televised memorial event the following year.

About a Pump

I had such terrible spasticity in my left ankle that my foot would actually rotate inward so that when I put pressure on it, it would move in a spraining motion. At Hurley, they had made braces for my legs, called AFOs (Ankle-Foot Orthotics). These kept my ankles from spraining and worked great for a while, but as time went on the spasticity in my left ankle became so bad that it would fight against the brace making it painful to wear, let alone walk in.

I've taken Baclofen orally since the early days at Hurley. Baclofen is a drug that works as a muscle relaxer as well as an anti-spastic agent. We had initially heard about the Baclofen Pump from Dr. Alpiner, who suggested that I would be a good candidate for it. He didn't push it and we were pretty much clueless. Anyway, several years removed from Hurley, I decided that I wanted to pursue this option.

The Baclofen Pump is a device that is used to deliver very small quantities of Baclofen directly into the spinal fluid. It consists of a metal pump that's surgically inserted under the covering of the abdominal muscles. The computerized pump stores and delivers the medication through a catheter into the spinal cord where the medication takes effect.

Anyway, I went down to a hospital in the Detroit area, where they were to run a trial on me to assess whether it relieved my spasticity. In order to perform the trial, they had to do a lumbar puncture, also known as a spinal tap. There were two doctors present. They had me on my side as they tried to perform the puncture. They missed three times, with each time being very painful, before they finally decided to do the procedure under x-ray, where they nailed it on the first try!

174

A couple hours afterward they had me on my feet to evaluate if the dose relieved my spasticity. It didn't. So they suggested that they keep me over night and they would try a higher dose tomorrow. Well that wasn't gonna happen! I'd had enough of these clowns playing their game of darts on my spine. Based on my experience, I didn't have any confidence in their ability to surgically install a screw into an apple, let alone a computerized pump into me.

The day after I returned home, I developed an excruciating headache that wouldn't quit. After suffering for what seemed like a week, but was actually two days, my parents took me to the emergency room. It seems headaches are a common side effect of a spinal tap. They hooked me up intravenously to caffeine. I used to joke and say that they had hooked me up to an espresso maker. Well, needless to say, my headache disappeared.

Tendon Release

Sometime later, I looked into having my tendon lengthened on my left foot. Dr. Alpiner had also recommended this earlier. When he had recommended the procedure, my spasticity in that foot wasn't that bad. I was progressing and didn't want to be sidelined with a cast. Dr. Alpiner was right about many things, but he was incredibly insensitive and irritating. So I changed doctors. Dr. Anthony Femminineo visited River Distant Hospital where I had done rehab, so I changed to started seeing him periodically. Eventually, I had the tendon lengthening procedure done by Dr. Kreis. When he cast it after the procedure, he cast it outward to compensate for the inward pull. Now my left foot points slightly outward, like a duck bill. But at least it doesn't hurt anymore. I had new ankle-foot orthosis made mainly because I had a tendency to hyperextend my legs when I walked and the braces prevented this.

Crippled Hands/Botox

My hands are without a doubt the most crippled and limiting part of my injury. With palm down, my left wrist deviates inward and some of my fingers swan neck backward. While at Hurley, they were so spastic that they would just ball up into fists and my thumbs would tuck inside. I would wear splints that were meant to keep my hands open. But I could only bear them for a short time, because of the immense pain that they caused.

When Sue started working with me at my parents' house, we had a mat table. Sue would set me on my knees and have me bend forward into a crawling position. With the spasticity, my tendency was to want to just use my fists. But Sue would take my hands, flatten them and have me bear weight on them. At first, this was so excruciating, that I'd scream in pain. With time, my hands were well stretched, and I was on the ground crawling. I was making genuine progress; my fine motor skills were absent, but I was doing well with larger movements.

Several years had passed. Sue wasn't working with me any longer and I was getting restless, wanting more use out of my hands. At Hurley, Dr. Alpiner used Botox injections in my left bicep, which worked quite well. Botox injections, while commonly used for cosmetic purposes, are effective in reducing muscle spasticity. I went from having my left arm in a kinked, kind of permanent half-flexed position, to being able to consciously straighten it. Although, after a while, the kink returned.

Dr. Alpiner had also done Botox injections in my hands, though the benefit wasn't as noticeable as in my arm. Anyway, I decided that I would see about getting another Botox injection in my right hand. The effects are supposed to wear off after three months, so I figured it wouldn't hurt. We found a doctor who specialized in the procedure. I had the injections done in my right hand only, because it's my dominant hand.

Not long after the procedure, my parents and I headed up to Frankenmuth Michigan to see Third Day and FFH in concert. The day following the concert, as the injections finally took effect, I realized that I had made a terrible mistake. It was difficult for me to make a fist, or grasp things, like a cup or even my walker. I had a fit and was freaking out. What had I done?! Of course, the effects wore off after a few months, but to this day my right hand is slightly more crippled than it was before the Botox injections.

Georgia/Florida

I earned my associates degree with honors from St. Clair County Community College in 2003. By that time, I had become disillusioned with psychology and its humanistic/man-centered approach. Meanwhile, our neighbor's two children had been healed of severe allergies. I had grown up two houses away from Shannon and Stephanie, and was well aware of how debilitating their allergies were. Though they both earned degrees from Port Huron High School, they had essentially been home schooled because they couldn't be around any perfume or cologne. They had gone to a church in Thomaston Georgia, which was called Pleasant Valley at the time. The church hosts *"Be in Health"* conferences, under the teaching of Pastor Henry Wright.

The teaching argued that the diseases we struggle with have spiritual roots, which if resolved, will result in physical healing. I had known Shannon and Stephanie's parents, Kevin and Marcia, to be solid Christians with discernment. Even after they had returned from the conference, with Shannon and Stephanie almost entirely

177

healed of their allergies, they were questioning some of the ministry's principles. They asked me if I had ever come across some of the teaching that they described. In fact, I had. While the focus of **The Bondage Breaker** had been almost entirely on spiritual freedom, many of the elements they described reminded me of it. So I lent them the book. They read it and came away comforted, having dots connected, assured that this was of God.

In late May of 2003, they were taking Stephanie back down to Georgia because she still had residual issues, while her brother Shannon had experienced a fuller level of healing.

They suggested that my parents and I ought to go. I had pointed out, and they knew that my disability was not a result of disease, but had happened in the natural realm as a result of a poor decision. But they were believing God for a creative miracle in my life. I know that God is able and I was eager for a miracle, as I was still chasing physical healing. Since I had been disillusioned with psychology, and have an obvious passion for theology, we decided that we'd take two weeks – one week for the conference and another week to look at Christian seminaries in Florida.

A week or so before we left for Georgia and Florida, while Laurie was walking with me, she was telling me about her half-sister, Luckette, who would have just turned 18. Laurie had a different biological father than Nicole and I. She's almost 12 years older and has always been a mother figure to me. She teases me that our Dad chose her, while he was stuck with me. One time Laurie was helping me exercise at the gym when she said, "I have three half-sisters and one half-brother. I looked at her and said in all seriousness, "I've never met your half-brother." She looked at me like "you can't be serious." We had a good laugh, as it slowly dawned on me that I was the half-brother she was referring to. But ultimately, that's a great complement to her. I don't think of her as my half-sister. As far as I'm concerned, she's always been my sister. Getting back to Luckette, the last Laurie had known, she was in Key Largo, Florida. She had never had any contact with her. She only knew that Luckette existed. Keep this in mind and you'll soon see its relevance.

We packed my handicapped accessible van and headed for Georgia. Meanwhile my mom had discovered that a childhood friend of hers, who had recently lost her husband, lived near our destination. Her town was the next one over. We actually had to pass her road to get to Thomaston. So while we were there my mom was able to catch up with and comfort her as she grieved.

We arrived the afternoon of Sunday May 25th, checked into the motel and headed over to the church, which was a little more than five minutes away from the motel. The church was not a traditional church. It was actually an old school and the conferences and services were held in the old gymnasium. Thank God Kevin, Marcia and Stephanie were there, because it had the feel of a cult. Even Kevin and Marcia admitted that when they first had gone down they thought, *"What have we gotten ourselves into?"*

We checked in, and then went over to a praise and worship service in the gym. Next we went through orientation, where we were given a notebook that consisted of teaching times as well as outlines of the teaching. Nothing seemed too unusual.

The next day we arrived at 8:30 in the morning for a half hour praise and worship service to start the day. Every morning started with praise and worship. It was definitely uplifting and helpful in getting our hearts prepared for the things of God. Still, I knew enough to use discernment and keep my wits about me. I had theological differences. But most of the teaching was in line with the things that I had already learned through **The Bondage Breaker.**

There were several different ministers who taught. In fact, though he did teach a little, I rarely saw Pastor Henry Wright.

Tuesday, after their teachings, the ministers started implementing the teachings. They began to have what I can only call mass deliverance sessions. There wasn't any grandstanding, no lying on of hands or speaking in tongues. The ministers simply began casting out evil spirits in the name of Jesus Christ of Nazareth. Of course we had to renounce and repent of sin whether ancestral or our own, lest the spirits have an opportunity to return. *"When an unclean spirit has gone out of a man, he passes through waterless places, seeking rest, and doesn't find it. Then he says, 'I will return into my house from which I came out,' and when he has come back, he finds it empty, swept, and put in order. Then he goes, and takes with himself seven other spirits more evil than he is, and they enter in and dwell there. The last state of that man becomes worse than the first... (Matthew 12:43-45a WEB)*

I saw confirmation that something supernatural was indeed happening. On one occasion, a man who had been sitting directly in front of us, charged at the minister on all fours, his hands and toes, growling like a dog. When the man was close enough that the minister saw what was happening, he calmly cast out the spirit of bestiality and the man returned to his senses. On another occasion, I noticed that a man in the back of the church went into a catatonic state, which is characterized by muscular rigidity, a mental stupor and a general unresponsiveness to the external world. The minister that was teaching didn't stop nor call attention to it, he simply kept teaching while others ministered to the man. Like I said, there wasn't any grandstanding or men calling attention to themselves. All was done in the name of Jesus.

In fact, after the teaching on the occult, during the deliverance session, my mother became extremely nauseated. She was nauseated to the point where she needed a trash bag into which she repeatedly gagged. Once again, without drawing attention, a minister attended to the personal needs of my mother. We knew that my grandmother had dabbled with occult practices. My mom said that during the ministry she had no appetite and the very thought of food made her ill. Yet immediately after the ministry session was over, when we returned to the school for lunch, her appetite returned and she ate.

Being raised Catholic, I had been baptized as an infant. I understood the intent behind this, but it bore little significance to me, because it wasn't my choice. So on Thursday May 29th of that year (2003), I was re-baptized in a swimming pool, near Pleasant Valley Church. It wasn't my intent to negate what had been done to me as an infant, but to fulfill it. Thankfully, my parents understood my heart in this matter. In fact, they were re-baptized as well!

Near the end of the week, as it was becoming increasingly apparent that God wasn't going to heal me with a creative or restorative miracle, I became depressed and started to question God. Since I had never actually sought Him in regards to the trip and the fact that I likely wouldn't have heard or obeyed Him if He had said no, was I outside of God's will?

We traveled down to Florida where we explored a couple of seminaries near Orlando. I learned that most seminaries only offer masters programs, which meant I would need a Bachelor's degree. Before heading home, we decided we would stop at Pensacola Christian College, which offered Bachelor's degrees in Biblical Studies. We left Orlando and on our way to Pensacola got caught up in a treacherous rainstorm. We couldn't see the road, so we tried to pull off at a rest area as soon as the storm started, but a semi-truck blocked that option.

It was only around 6 pm, but the storm was so bad and didn't show any signs of letting up, so we decided we might as well try to find a room for the night. We pulled off at the first exit we could, exit 427; Lake City. We pulled into a motel off the expressway, but it seemed others had had the same idea, as the motel was booked. There was a Bob Evans across the street, so I suggested that we stop in for dessert and see if the storm would let up any. After all, it was early and we were still quite a distance away from Pensacola.

We entered the restaurant, where we were seated in the non-smoking section. Our waitress was an attractive young blonde with blue/green eyes, so of course I looked at her name tag in case I wanted to flirt with her. Then I exclaimed, "Mom, Luckette!" My mom asked the young lady what her name was. With a southern accent, she replied, "Luckette Wilson." Laurie's maiden name was Wilson. This was her half-sister!

Mom called Laurie's house on the cell phone, but she wasn't home. Steve answered, so my mom told Steve to have her call when she got in. When she called back, my mom answered and said, "We have somebody who wants to talk to you." We handed the phone to Luckette and she said bluntly, "Hi Laurie, this is your sister Luckette." I couldn't hear Laurie's response, but my mom reported that she said something like, "Yeah, I understand that this is Luckette. But what are you doing with my family?" They exchanged information.

I know this wasn't about me, but I received assurance that I was right where God wanted me. Ultimately though, I decided that Pensacola Christian College wasn't the right place for me. Since the student population was so large, I saw myself getting lost in a sea of faces.

ITC

Later on, in the summer of 2003, I attended Indian Trails Camp for the first time. Located in Grand Rapids, Michigan, Indian Trails is a camp for people with disabilities. When we first arrived, my parents and I were confronted with a whole new perspective, as most of the campers were in far worse shape than I was. Many lacked the ability to communicate verbally. My parents were questioning what kind of time I'd have at the camp, when a man in a scooter pulled up and said, "Hi, my name's Jim. Do you play euchre?" My parents thought, well Ryan will be alright; at least he'll have somebody to play cards and shoot the breeze with.

Five minutes later we were down at my cabin getting me unpacked and meeting my counselors, when the same man once again pulled up in his scooter and said, "Hi, my name's Jim. Do you play euchre?" My parents thought, *"Great, the one camper who approached us didn't remember that he'd met us five minutes ago."* It had been five years since the crash and my parents had scarcely left my side. Now that they were about to leave me at camp, they were understandably worried. They asked me if I was going to be alright. I was unsure myself, but I assured them that I would be. They reminded me more than once if I had any problems I should call them. I guess that after they left, they both cried.

Camp turned out to be the most fun I had had since the crash. I learned that even though many couldn't communicate verbally, they could still communicate and desired to know and be known; to develop friendships. It's a very rewarding experience to connect with people who the world ignores and often writes off as worthless. These people were just like me! They too were trapped in bodies, with souls that given the opportunity would burst forth and light up a life. The counselors are blessed with the opportunity to have their

183

lives lit. I have the privilege of not only sharing this blessing, but being a blessing myself with the ability to light up lives.

As of this writing, I've attended Indian Trails Camp for a week every summer since my first experience in 2003. I've had many experiences, but after being there in the summer of 2011, I finally wrote about camp for another ministry that actually didn't pick up the piece. Nevertheless, I shared it with several of the counselors as well as a few fellow campers via Facebook. It follows;

7/21/11

For 8 summers now I have attended Indian Trails Camp. Located in Grand Rapids, Michigan, ITC is a camp whose mission is to provide individuals with disabilities an enriched life experience through recreation, advocacy and meaningful relationships. It's a place where people generally considered outcasts by society, find affinity, love and acceptance. The amazing thing is that the love and acceptance come not only from fellow campers, but from the camp counselors, who are almost entirely made up of college students. Their acceptance of us as human beings, worthy of dignity, respect and attention is simply astonishing. I'm sure that the counselors are more, or at least equally affected by the campers, who generally display appreciation and joy in the midst of their circumstances.

I am writing as one who is among the least disabled campers, one who always comes away with a new appreciation for life. Something that I've found is that most of the campers are fully aware of what's going on around them, but many have difficulty communicating; beautiful souls trapped in broken bodies. It's a shame that most of the

184

world misses this, but I am thankful for those who take advantage of the opportunity to connect. I've also been blessed with this opportunity.

This summer, one camp friend of mine, who has difficulty communicating and who is comparatively much more disabled than me, conveyed that he was sorry that I had gotten in a crash. Being slightly familiar with Craig's story, but not recalling, I asked, "Weren't you in a car accident Craig?" He replied, "Yeah…, I…was…in…my…mother's…womb." Such is the spirit of most campers; we are hurting people, who hate to see others hurt.

Though many who attend are Christians, it is not a Christian camp. So I have fun witnessing to people, mainly the counselors, by sharing my testimony. By the end of the week, I have made many new friends, but there are also those who stand far off. Not because they have rejected me, but because they reject the Gospel.

Major Choice

Since I enjoy writing, I thought that I would pursue a Bachelor's degree in journalism, so I enrolled at Oakland University in Rochester Hills, Michigan for the fall semester in 2004. It was a little more than an hour commute from Port Huron. My poor Dad and I would get up at 6 am to get ready and leave for school about 8. I usually slept on the way there. Sometimes I slept on the way back. We typically didn't get home until after 7 pm. Meanwhile, my dad was awake the whole day.

The first semester, without seeing a counselor in the journalism department, I took Introduction to Spanish and Introduction to the Middle East, as the counselor I did see had indicated that a semester of a foreign language was a prerequisite for a degree in journalism and the Intro to the ME class covered another prerequisite.

Before the next semester, winter 05, I saw a counselor in the Journalism Department and she recommended I take JRN 200, News Writing, which was also a prerequisite. I registered for that course and a course in British Literature. After two classes of each, it became apparent that both courses were very demanding. One girl I had met also had both classes; she dropped the course in Journalism, while I dropped the course in British Literature. As I was saying, the journalism class was very involved and I quickly realized that journalism was more than just writing. The task that I found most daunting, with my speech impairment, was interviewing. I so hated interviewing people that, while I passed the class with a low A, I was left doubting whether journalism was the path for me.

Meanwhile, during the summer of 2005, it was announced that the University of Michigan Flint was partnering with St. Clair County Community College's university center to offer Bachelor degrees in psychology. With my doubts about journalism and the realization of just how taxing the commute to OU was on my dad, I reevaluated my aversion to psychology and decided that I'd redeem what I could from the science. I was able to take most of the classes at SC4, but the degree required that I take two laboratory classes on their campus, so I had to commute to Flint for them, as well for as another semester of Spanish.

Embracing the Call

I AM NOT eloquent; in fact, I still have noticeable speech impairment. But it was becoming clear that the Lord had called me to share my story. I got my start speaking in churches. I was comfortable there because it was a friendly environment where I could share my faith freely. I first spoke at Immanuel in Roseville at the invitation of Pastor Tom. Others may have viewed it differently, but according to my assessment, it was a disaster. I didn't have a video nor did I use an outline. Before I spoke, I thought, *"I lived it, I should be able to talk about it."* But when I was up there in front of everybody, I forgot almost everything I had planned to say. Also, at that point I wasn't aware that Geoff had been with me, so that dimension hadn't been added yet. Fortunately, my mom was with me and she kept me on track. Afterwards, Pastor Tom suggested I create an outline to keep me on point.

Months prior to the trip to Georgia, in the winter of 2003, I was contacted by Marcy, a D.A.R.E. Officer who invited me to come and share my message with the D.A.R.E. board. Well, I could see where this was heading; there would be a desire for me to speak at public schools in the area, and maybe beyond. Honestly, I was uncomfortable with the thought. I found an audience in the church and that's where I desired to stay. I was comfortable "preaching to the choir," as the cliché goes. Nevertheless, I agreed to share my message intending to make my faith the centerpiece in order to scare off any interest. In that speech, I talked about my faith more than I had in any previous presentation. My dad even predicted I would get negative feedback because it would be perceived as overly "religious."

A week later, I received 14 reviews with only one taking note of the "religious overtones." Still, there would be no direct partnership with D.A.R.E. I thought I had dodged a bullet, but the Lord had other plans. Marcy had been impressed with the presentation and she contacted an acquaintance of hers about it. Her acquaintance was Gordie, a Health Instructor at Port Huron Northern High School (PHN). He in turn contacted me and asked if I'd be willing to speak to his classes. Well, I was not one to turn down speaking invitations, especially with a suspicion that God was involved. So I agreed to come in.

I first spoke during a day in which parent-teacher conferences had shaken the hours up so that the 1st, 2nd, and 3rd hour classes were shifted to the afternoon. My mom and I spoke in the library to these first three hours consecutively one afternoon. I refrained from outright sharing my faith. Although, I did make casual references, and at the end of each class I handed out copies of my testimony. I was slated to speak to the 4th, 5th, and 6th hour classes in the classroom the next day. When I arrived, apparently after a discussion with his Curriculum Director, Gordie expressed some concern about the testimonies I handed out and asked me to refrain from handing them out.

I did, but in my heart I was venting at the Lord, *"See Lord, this is why I didn't want to do public venues. I knew that they would censor the message!"* So I just shared the message regarding drinking and driving with casual references to my faith. A couple days later, I received a phone call from Betty, a psychology teacher at Port Huron High

School (PHHS), my alma mater. She told me that her daughter had heard my presentation and shared it with her, which prompted her to ask if we'd come and speak to her classes. Since it takes a lot to get me ready, we'd only be able to do her afternoon classes. When we arrived, I showed her my testimony, explained what had happened at PHN, and asked if it would be alright to hand out copies. Betty said yes, that her daughter had brought home a copy and that she'd take any heat that resulted from them.

Even so, a difference emerged; Gordie went out of his way to pursue me to speak, while if I wanted to speak at PHHS, I generally had to pursue the opportunity. Although from 2008 through 2010, there was a Health Teacher at PHHS, named Karla, who had heard about me from Gordie and she invited me to come in to speak to her classes. I was also invited back to speak at PHHS by Tricia on Wednesday, May 25th 2016.

I am unsure how long my speaking career will continue. However, I have chosen to write the following in the present rather than past tense.

With my mom as my sidekick, the presentations typically go like this; I have the teacher give me a brief introduction. Then I launch into the presentation, and without fail, as soon as I began to speak I seem to have everyone's undivided attention. While I once considered my speech impairment a weakness, God uses it to capture the attention of the audience with the realization that they are going to have to pay careful attention if they are to understand the message. I explain that when I was 19 years old, a friend and I had gone to Canada to party at a bar, but that we never made it back to the States that night; we were in car crash. My friend's neck was broken upon impact and he died instantly. Myself, I was tossed from

189

the vehicle and into a coma where I teetered between life and death for just under a month.

I share the dire predictions of the doctors and briefly mention how when I did wake-up, I was unable to do anything; I couldn't speak, I couldn't eat, I couldn't move any of my limbs or lift my head. I was told that I had suffered a traumatic brain injury as a result of a car crash. I felt like I was trapped in a prison of my own making.

I mention how I had to learn almost everything over again, that in my mind I knew how to do, but my body wouldn't cooperate. For example, I had all my vocabulary but getting my tongue to the point where it would form the words was a long arduous process. Then we show a 10-minute video we made so that they can get more familiar with me and my situation.

The video starts off with pictures of me, mostly my graduation pictures, and then pans over to some empty alcoholic beverage containers, some pills and some oregano, which resembles marijuana. This scene plays with Creed's *"My Own Prison"* as background music. Next it cuts to some video of my truck, as it was after the crash; totaled, while *"The Hard Way"* by DC Talk appropriately plays with these lyrics; "Some people have to learn the hard way. I guess I'm the kind of guy who has to find out for myself. I had to learn the hard way Father. I'm on my knees and I'm crying for help."[30]

Then it switches over to some video of my rehabilitation; first at Hurley where I really struggled, with the sad *"He's My Son"* by Mark Schultz playing. Then some of me at River District Hospital and my home, as the more hopeful *"No Doubt"* by Petra plays. Next, the video switches over to a cemetery and pans over several gravestones. Finally, the video cuts to me in my bedroom where I say, "In July of

1998 I was in a drinking and driving accident. As with most of these tragedies, this one too ends up in the cemetery. My friend Geoff Harris was killed upon impact. I spent just under a month in a coma and I've been going through extensive therapy the past few (I should have said several) years. I hope and pray that this has an impact upon all who watch it. Thank you and God bless."

After the video, I tell how just like most of them, I too thought that I was invincible, but that the fatality rate is 100%. All of us will die! I never thought that this would happen to me. My line of thought before the crash was, *"Yeah, it was too bad that it happened to that guy, but it will never happen to me."* I never thought about the consequences of my actions. Our lives are shaped by the choices we make and these choices affect more people than we ever know. Most of my choices were selfish; I gave little thought to how others might be affected.

Then raising my crippled hands for all to see, I stress how real all this is. I tell them that we reap what we sow. Through drug and alcohol abuse I sowed destruction into my body and as a result, I reaped a harvest of that destruction. Next, I take an unexpected approach for someone in my position. I tell them that I am not naïve; I realize that, when of age, most of them will choose to drink, if they don't already. I do not condemn alcohol any more than I condemn automobiles. Alcohol, in and of itself is not evil, but overindulgence and irresponsible decisions can be deadly. I ask that when they do drink, to do so in moderation and be responsible, that they plan ahead. I remind them to count the costs, asking if a night of partying is worth a lifetime of suffering.

Then I seek to identify with the students, assuring them that I was once where they're at and I understand the powerful impact of peer pressure. When tragedy strikes, you find out who your friends are. Ultimately, none of my friends remained there for me, but it was my family who had my back. Next, I point to the fact that most of the things that they take for granted, I am unable to do, and it's humiliating. Things like putting clothes on, shaving, showering and many other things that they do without thought. I say that they may have been able to tell by my selection of music on the video, that I am a man of faith. I emphasize that it's this faith that gives me the courage and confidence to speak to them.

Then, I throw it to my mom, and she talks about how Geoff was only 17. How I didn't know he'd been with me for two and a half years, because the doctors and psychologists had advised them not to share this information with me. Then she shows them the ABC chart, and explains how difficult it was for me to communicate. She shares the details of my fight with my sister, Nikki —how she had borrowed a shirt of mine without asking, so I lit into her. After exchanging some heated words, she yelled, "I hate you!" I responded in the like and she returned to California without us reconciling. Later, my mom would have to call her and tell her that I had been in a car crash and wasn't expected to live. She uses this story to warn the kids to be careful what words you leave a loved one with, because those could be last words they hear from you.

My mom brings the important perspective of a mother who has witnessed her son suffer as a result of a bad decision. After her talk, I invite questions and answers. This is my favorite time because I get to go off script and show flashes of wit and humor. I tell the audience not to be shy, because I'm not. After Q & A, the teacher wraps it up.

So, as unwilling as I was initially to do public venues, the Lord had taken me to a new level. I experience a spiritual high whenever I share my story and I'm amazed that God has given me a platform from which I am able to not only save lives, but also introduce people to the saving Gospel of Jesus Christ. I was taken from a level where I'd merely accepted my affliction to a place where I now embraced it. Second Corinthians 12:9 became my life verse; *"But he said to me, 'My grace is sufficient for you, for my power is made perfect in weakness.' Therefore I will boast all the more gladly of my weaknesses, so that the power of Christ may rest upon me."* (ESV) I am astounded at how God uses my weakness as I see the power of Christ rest on me and lives changed. And this was only the beginning!

Interestingly, without sharing my experience at PHN with him, my friend Shannon, who I wrote about earlier in the subsection **Florida/George** of the **Back to Life** section, asked me if I would like him to build a website for me. This was an option I had never even considered. Through it, God provided a way for me to bring not only my testimony where it was formerly unwelcome, but the Gospel itself. The Lord had provided a Trojan horse. Of course, it would be the responsibility of each individual to take the time to check out the site, but I would do my best with my God given charm and wit to encourage them to.

My Website

My buddy Shannon had broached the subject of a website during the summer of 2003. He was on the brink of earning a Bachelor of Fine Arts in Digital Arts at Bowling Green State University in Bowling Green, Ohio. Shannon and some friends of his had formed a web design company called NomadicaMedia. So during the fall and winter of 03-04, he and I communicated primarily via e-mail.

He instructed me to purchase a domain name through godaddy.com. At that point, I had never heard of the currently popular domain registrar. I registered the name ryankrafftproject.com, since I knew this was never about me. Shannon's buddy, Luke, had access to a server that sponsored faith-based sites free of charge, and he was kind enough to see to it that the server would sponsor my site.

I provided pictures, written content, and the song *"Mistakes"* by Kutless, which they incorporated into the site. When I inquired about the site for this writing, Shannon informed me that his friend Steve was responsible for the unique design. And it was unique. I hadn't t seen anything like it nor have I since. The site opened to a page that looked like the middle of a journal with the previous pages torn out. It resembled the turning point in my life that the crash had become. The name of the site, RyanKrafft/Project, sat in a kind of rustic brown color on top of the page, with a quarter of a picture of my smashed up truck resting below. Proverbs 16:18 was placed below the picture; it read *"Pride goes before destruction, a haughty heart before a fall."* *(NIV)* I felt that this verse captured my attitude of invincibility prior to the crash. Finally, in the same rustic brown, placed in the center of the page was the word ENTER, enticing the user to enter the site through the porthole that the page served as.

After the user clicked on ENTER the actual site would pop up. I later learned that some users' pop-up blockers actually prevented them from entering the site. Once they entered, the first thing the user saw was the introduction page that looked like a slightly aged piece of paper that had been torn out of a notebook. The rest of the site took on a similar look, giving the reader the impression that he or she had stumbled upon an old journal.

In my original draft of this book, I went into considerable detail describing the website design. And impressive though it was, it was only a website. I also originally shared the content of the site, but my editor, Jill, noted that much of the content mirrored what I had already written in this book, so it wasn't necessary to include it. However, my website does contain information not shared in this book, so I encourage you to check it out.

Now I was fully expecting to pay at least a couple hundred bucks for the work that Shannon and his team did on the site. But when it was finished, Shannon said that it was pro bono (i.e. free). This was an incredible blessing to me. Shannon and I kept contact as I tweaked the wording of the content and added new dimensions to the site. I added the Current Update section, and I required assistance changing the content every few months.

In order to allow me to share my website with others in an easy manner, I created web invites. These are little slips of paper with the website address and the introductory sentences on them. "One fate-filled night after drinking with some friends at a bar in Canada, I put the keys in the ignition of my truck, intending to drive home. That decision would dramatically change my life forever and ultimately launch me on a journey in which I have faced trials, tribulations, doubts and demons. As well as these, I invite you to share in my triumph, revolution of the soul, calling, new relationships and some profound wisdom."

During the summer of 2006, while at the Krafft family reunion, I was talking with my cousin, Dave. I learned that he's a Web Designer and at that time he was working at a place called Elemental, in Troy, Michigan. He was asking me about my site, how much it cost to design and upkeep. I said, "I had it done for free and so far the upkeep has been free as well!" Dave replied, "Well I can't beat that! But if you need any help, let me know and I'll match it."

Not four months later Shannon let me know that he was getting busy, and that I was going to have to find someone else to help me with the site. I thanked him for all his hard work, and remembering Dave, thought to myself, *"Wow God! Good looking out!"* Since I had the main content of the site tweaked to my liking, the only help I really needed was with the Current Update section. So Dave came up one afternoon, set me up with the necessary programs and taught me enough about HTML (i.e. web language), that I was able to do the updates myself.

Eventually, I had Dave remove the song *"Mistakes"* by Kutless. It correlated so well with my story that people who hadn't met me would ask if that was me singing or if I wrote the song. So I figured to avoid confusion, it would be best to just remove it.

Skip ahead 7 years. The day after the family reunion in the fall of 2013, Dave e-mailed me saying that he wanted to talk to me about my website at the reunion, but that I had been "sleeping like a boss."

It's true; I had eaten too much, so I tilted my power chair back and dozed off. Though I don't take advantage often, clocking out almost wherever I want is one advantage of being disabled. Anyway, he asked if I had ever heard of Word Press. I hadn't. He explained that it was an alternative to HTML that would be easier for me to use. Still being pretty much HTML illiterate, easier sounded great to me. But to implement Word Press he'd have to redesign my site.

I figured after ten years it was about time for a fresh design. So I gave him the go ahead. With Dave living in Royal Oak and me spending most of winter in Florida, we communicated via e-mail. I wasn't able to get a hold of Luke, so I had to purchase a different server to host my site. Through godaddy.com, I purchased a new server that was made to host Word Press. I also picked the template that Dave used to design the sight anew.

The newly designed site went live on May 27th, 2014 and Dave hooked me up with the administration login information the next day. The new design was very classy, but it still took me a couple of days to let go of the old and adjust to the new. I am going to refrain from describing it because it's more basic and I hope to have the site still available for the reader to view under the URL www.ryankrafftproject.com

Dave, working under his freelance business, www.digitalmixture.com, did a phenomenal job. Putting in between $1500-2000 worth of work into my site, I simply can't describe how appreciative I am to him for giving me the "family discount." As a way to show my appreciation, I am using this space to say, if you should ever have any web design needs, please throw your business my cousin's way by contacting him through the website address above.

Back to Life Again

Time With an Old Friend

IN 2002, I was taking an American history course at St. Clair County Community College. One of my friends from high school was also in the class. One afternoon he asked if he could talk with me after class. So we talked, he apologized for not being there for me in my time of need and said that he'd like to get together.

When we did, I learned that he had also been in a car crash in which he also had been the drunk driver. He had injured his hip badly, but on the whole that was the extent of his injuries. However, he was now dealing with the legal ramifications of the ordeal. He had his license revoked and was on probation.

As part of his probation, the authorities recommended that he attend Alcoholics Anonymous (AA). Alcoholics Anonymous is a 12-step program intended to liberate alcoholics from the bondage of alcoholism. The 3rd step encourages participants to make a decision to turn their will and their lives over to the care of "God *as they understand him.*" Well, my buddy was wise enough to know that if he was to have any understanding of God, he'd best turn to the God of the Bible, lest he make an idol for himself, like many, if not most participants do.

We enjoyed fellowship for several months. He went to Bible study with me and I hooked him up with a copy of *The Bondage Breaker* by Neil Anderson. We had many great conversations regarding the faith. Then his girlfriend came home from school. I met her and I liked her, but I discerned a religious spirit about her, which as I indicated earlier, typically exhibits itself in self-righteousness. To be clear, I do not use the term self-righteous as an insult. Rather, I use the team to convey a theological reality, probably best summarized in Romans 10:3, *"For they being ignorant of God's righteousness, and seeking to* **establish their own righteousness***, have not submitted to the righteousness of God."* (*NKJV* **emphasis added**)

Anyway, being young and zealous for the faith, one evening without tact, I tried to reveal the futility of religion. Essentially, I attacked her religious spirit. Without establishing the standard of good I was referring to as righteousness that's acceptable to God (ultimate goodness), I cut corners, fouled up and pushed her deeper into a defensive position of self-righteousness. I asked without follow up, "You think you're pretty good, don't ya?" To which she replied smugly, "Yup!"

I know my friend knew that my intentions were good. But needless to say, you can't come between a guy and his girlfriend, especially one that would eventually become his wife! I wrote a letter of apology for my overzealousness and tactless approach, but I didn't apologize for the biblical assessment of the human race – that mankind is both noble and wretched. We are noble, because we're created in the image of God, and yet wretched, because we are born fallen and alienated from Him. Apparently my letter wasn't well received, as I only saw my friend a couple more times.

"John"

One of my best friends growing up had joined the army and was off before I came out of the coma. Meanwhile in 2003, his older brother had moved back home to Michigan from Florida. I will be using the pseudonym John to refer to my friend, as I haven't obtained his permission, nor do I think he'd appreciate me writing about him, but he is an important part of my journey. In Florida, John was a chemist who worked for a well-known corporation and held several patents. It is my understanding that he struggled with alcoholism, so his wife, hoping that being close to the family would help, moved back home to Michigan. Several months later John quit his job, and followed his wife back home to Michigan.

Unfortunately, her hopes that being close to family would help John kick alcoholism didn't happen. Having had enough of watching John self-destruct, his wife filed for divorce in 2004.

John and I started hanging out shortly after he moved back to town in 03. It didn't take long for me to delve into faith, and I could tell that he was initially uncomfortable. John had gone to AA, but as I noted before AA is not a Christian group. Though many Christians attend AA, very few have ever been converted to Christianity because of AA. Anyway, I watched a short movie with John that I knew would open up an opportunity for me to evangelize. Yeah, you could say that I set him up.

After the movie, I asked him a pointed question. "So John, have you been born again?" He replied, "I have my own thoughts and questions about that." I persisted, "What kind of questions?" He resorted to that legitimate, but sidestepping question that I mentioned earlier in **Consequences**. "What about those who've never heard the Gospel?" At this point I didn't feel adequate to answer this question, but uncannily I had just finished reading a booklet from RBC Ministries titled, *"What About Those Who Have Never Heard?"* There was the question, almost identical to the way John asked it, so I retrieved the booklet and gave it to John.

As John and I started to develop a tighter friendship, I continued sharing my faith. Even though he didn't initially have saving faith, John was always very respectful and willing to converse about such things. I taught John how to play chess and it didn't seem long before the student was whipping up on the teacher. With a Bachelor's of Science in Chemistry, and his experience in research and development, John was very intelligent. His intelligence often got in the way of the simplicity of faith. Not only did John and I often engage in discussions about faith when in one another's company, but we also carried on the conversation via e-mail. The conversation was by no means consistent, because John would frequently fall off the grid as result of alcoholic binges. Nevertheless, it quickly became apparent that John was trying to engage God in some kind of intellectual exercise, trying to figure Him out as if God were some kind of puzzle to be solved. I moved quickly to dispel such a task. Rising to the level of John's vocabulary, I wrote, "It's futile for a finite mind to try and wrap itself around the infinite God. John, God is not some kind of puzzle to be solved or a Being that you can match wits with, if that were possible, He would no longer be God."

Nevertheless, John continued with this intellectual exercise for quite some time. While not always applying it, he was always very receptive to what I had to say and the resources I gave him. I gave him a Bible, copies of *The Case for Christ* and *The Case for Faith*, by Lee Strobel, as well as a copy of *The Bondage Breaker*, hoping to help him conquer his struggle with alcoholism. John read these things and was reading the Bible. I could see his heart softening. In 2006, I lent him my copy of the newly released nonfiction book *"Epicenter,"* by Joel C. Rosenberg. In *"Epicenter,"* Rosenberg lays out a clear case on how the rebirth of Israel, on May 16th 1948, was a clear fulfillment of Bible prophecy and how end times prophecy centers around the existence of Israel. Thus, Israel is the epicenter.

Rosenberg's writing was so clear and concise, as well as intellectually engaging, that John, being fully convinced of the authenticity of the Bible, finally gave in. He put his trust in Jesus alone and had a rebirth experience. But John was quick to put God to the test regarding his alcohol addiction. John expressed disappointment and frustration with me that God hadn't taken away his addiction. John has continued to struggle with alcoholism and has been in and out of rehab facilities frequently. Honestly, I saw him more before he got saved. But I know that it's not about me. In September of 2012, I received an unexpected phone call from John. He apologized and confessed some sin in his life beyond his obvious struggle with alcoholism. John also expressed doubt about his salvation. I assured him that despite his failures, if he was trusting in Christ alone, he was saved. I reminded him how the apostle Paul called the Corinthian believers' saints, when they acted anything but saintly. John, you're a saint!

Assuring someone of their salvation isn't something I'd normally do. But I knew that John grasped the gospel not only with his mind, but also with his heart and soul, because he had been exposed to many of the same teachings that I had been. Apart from Christ, in the depths of my being, I know that I am a wretch. So by reassuring John of his position before God, I was also reassuring myself. However, as I shared in **Becoming,** we are called to work out our salvation by participating with God in our sanctification. My desire and prayer for John is that he will fully submit to God, allowing the

Spirit to do His transformational work, so that John can live in the freedom He has in Christ.

When I pray for others, I tend to examine myself as well. While praying for John to be unshackled from the bondage of alcoholism, I am all too aware of my own shortcomings. The symptoms of John's sins are visible and many of us look down on those who struggle with substance addiction. I've heard it said and I have even said it myself, "John's an intelligent, handsome guy with a great education; it's too bad he's an alcoholic." I don't like negative labels because they tend to box a person in and reinforce their negative behavior and identity. It's revealing that you'll likely never hear such a statement as "So and so has so much going for them, it's too bad they're a pervert, or a glutton, or greedy, or racist, et cetera…" We all have sin issues and areas of weakness that need to be overcome as we become who we are in Christ. John's story isn't over yet!

Performing Arts Center

In November of 2005, Gordie, the health teacher whose classes I had been speaking to on a regular basis, suggested I speak in the new performing arts center that had been built, because there wasn't a time-split for parent/teacher conferences and he didn't want his morning classes to miss out. We would sacrifice the intimacy of the classroom, but we'd be able to do all the classes at once. As I replied at the time, "The performing arts center sounds better than getting out of bed earlier." I loved it! It was so much easier to give the presentation once rather than numerous times.

Maria Teresa

In August of 2005, I began chatting with Maria Teresa. I had met Maria on a Christian website. She didn't have a picture on her profile. Nevertheless, I was attracted to her profile and the genuine character that she portrayed with written words. Maria was Puerto Rican, and she still lived in Puerto Rico. She knew some English and since I had recently taken a Spanish class, I felt comfortable chatting with and learning from her and her from me.

We used to make chat dates that I anxiously looked forward to. On several occasions, I had to laugh at our miscommunications. Once she told me that her father was a shepherd. I thought for a moment, *"I didn't realize there were sheep herders in Puerto Rico."* Then the context hit me, "Oh, you mean a pastor!" "Yes a pastor," she replied. On another occasion, I had written the popular mistranslation "mono y mono," intending to say that I can't wait to meet you one-on-one or face to face. She had a good laugh, because in the way I used it, the phrase meant "monkey and monkey." In Spanish I literally wrote, "I can't wait to meet you monkey and monkey."

Yes, my parents and I had made plans to vacation for a week in Puerto Rico, during the spring of 2006. My mom, who's always up for an adventure, was easily talked into it. She even made all the arrangements! We were to stay at the Paradisus, an all-inclusive resort that was located in Rio Grande, which is about 25 miles east of San Juan. About 3 months before we left, I took a spill.

A Fall

On the Thursday morning of February 9th 2006, my sister Laurie was walking with me around the house. I was using a new black walker that was taller and made of steel. As the front wheels got caught up on a rug, I tumbled forward to the ground. I was so tired that day, I just wanted to lay there. But when I heard my dad and sister flipping out, asking me if I was okay, I knew that I must've sustained some damage from the fall. I opened my eyes and saw a small pool of blood. Apparently I had split my lip open on the walker or the floor. They rushed me to Port Huron Hospital's emergency room and the ER doctor put 7 stitches on the outside of my lip.

When I arrived home, I remarked to Laurie that it felt funny chewing on the stitches. She peeled my lip back and saw that I hadn't been chewing on the stitches. There was more damage on the inside of my lip. I had been chewing on my flesh! So we loaded back up and returned to the ER. After the ER doctor tried to justify his oversight by saying I didn't really need stitches on the inside, he put 3 more stitches on the inside of my lip.

When you're a toddler learning to walk, and you fall on your face from about 2 feet off the ground, little damage is done. But when you're a grown man and you fall on your face from 6 feet, considerable damage can occur. And of course my hands were occupied on the walker. Regardless, I tend to break falls with my head rather than my hands because my reaction time is slow. Yeah, by the time I even consider putting my hands out, I'm already on the floor. It's a complete afterthought.

To this day, I still have the semblance of a fat lip. My top lip sags a little lower on the right side. It's barely noticeable, but of course this is the first thing I see when I look in the mirror, or at a picture of myself. Why am I so quick to notice and focus in on the flaws in my appearance? Am I alone in this? Somehow I doubt it.

NailPoint

In March of 2006, I had seen a poster for a concert by a local rock band known at the time as NailPoint Payment, later shortened to NailPoint. I almost immediately recognized two of the members as guys that were in my 6th grade class. I had lost track of Jeff and Mark after intermediate school because they went to Port Huron Northern, while I went to Port Huron High.

I contacted them via e-mail from their website, dropping my website on them at the same time. They both remembered me, and were surprised to hear about the crash, but praised God with me for the work He was doing in and through me. They invited me out to one of their concerts, which I went to a couple of weeks after our exchange. I was also invited to give my testimony at one of their concerts.

Puerto Rico

On May 17th of that year, we arrived in Puerto Rico. We had arranged for a rental car. I remember that the young lady who picked us up in the rental car was very attractive. I sat in the passenger seat next to her and we chatted and flirted with one another. She was fluent in English and Spanish. She had said of speaking both languages "¡Es fácil!" (It's easy)! I replied, "¡Si, es fácil para ti, pero para mí, es muy difícil!" (Yes, it's easy for you, but it's very difficult for me!) When we dropped her off at the car rental place, I gave her a web invite. I had long since learned that my website was straight forward enough to endear the real, but make others feel uncomfortable, as well as engendering hostility from those opposed to the Gospel.

When we arrived at the Paradisus and finally relaxed, we were taken aback at the beauty of our surroundings. My parents were comparing it to Hawaii. The resort was very accommodating. I became quick friends with one of the employees there named, Nefdavid. Since I was physically unable to take advantage of a lot that the resort had to offer, on one of his lunch breaks he took me all over the resort and its adjoining beach on a golf cart.

Not long after we arrived at the resort, I called Maria and we made plans. Later in the week she was to come to the resort. I had received a couple pictures from Maria and she seemed attractive. The day of our meeting, as I waited, I saw two attractive young women and a man approaching the resort and it occurred to me that one of young women might be Maria. Sure enough, Maria had come with her sister, Natalia, and brother-in-law, Boris. Maria was more gorgeous than I had imagined! She had dark hair with beautiful brown eyes, that nice tan Puerto Rican complexion and a perfect figure.

We showed the three of them around the resort. Then Maria rode with us as we followed Boris and Natalia into Viejo San Juan (Old San Juan). We had dinner at The Hard Rock Café. Afterwards Boris, who spoke English better than the girls, led us on a tour of San Juan. Having a native lead us on a tour was a great experience. Before we parted company, we made plans to go to Maria's house to meet her parents and enjoy dinner together.

Three days later, my parents and I set off for Maria's house in Arroyo. Arroyo, Puerto Rico is on the south side of the island. It was about a 3-hour drive from Rio Grande. As we were taken in by the intoxicating beauty of the countryside, for the first time it occurred to us that we forgot to bring our camcorder. Not just to Arroyo, but to Puerto Rico altogether. Funny story, we stopped at a Wal-Mart on our way, not to purchase a camcorder, but to use the bathroom. Well me, being confident of my Spanish asked, "¿Cuándo es el baño?" Later, I had to laugh at myself as it occurred to me that I had slaughtered the question. I asked, "When *is* the bathroom?" Instead of, "¿Dónde está el baño?" (Where is the bathroom?)

We met up with Maria at an agreed upon location, which I don't remember, but it was about 15 miles away from her house. We followed her to her home from there. She lived in a nice ranch style home with her parents, Marcos and Luz Delia. Natalia and Boris were also there, and we enjoyed a wonderful meal together as everyone got to know each other. After dinner, her other sister Brendie and her husband Roy showed up to meet us. Roy spoke better English than Boris, and I thought Boris spoke it rather well for a second language!

Before we left, I think Maria and I were coming to the realization that we were worlds apart. She wasn't interested in leaving Puerto Rico, and me, with my support system back home, couldn't think about leaving Michigan. Before we left, her Dad, Marcos, who was a pastor of a Baptist Church, gave me a dual language Bible, English and Spanish. Maria led us back to where she had met up with us earlier that day.

It came time to leave, so we drove back to the rental car place and I was hoping that the same young lady that drove us before would be with us again. Not so. I asked my parents about her and they said that she was working on the computer. Okay, I thought, maybe she's busy and has contacted me via e-mail. But there wasn't an e-mail from her awaiting me when I got home. As I wrote earlier, my website is straightforward and I can only assume it made her uncomfortable. Of course, there are other possibilities, but this wasn't the first or the last time this happened.

Church

As you can tell, being one that was *"born again, not of perishable seed but of imperishable, through the living and abiding word of God." (1 Peter 1:23 ESV),* I have a passion for the Word of God. So after attending a church for most of my life, which has a heavy focus on sacraments, I found a church whose main focus was the Bible. Although I have many theological and doctrinal disagreements with Catholicism, I am not going to use space to highlight what I perceive as errors within the Catholic Church. Besides, the knowledgeable Catholic should have already perceived some of my differences. Neither am I going to be an ecumenical bridge between Catholics and Evangelicals. The chasm is too great and there is spiritual arrogance on both sides. Also, as of this writing, I still attend the Catholic Church that I grew up in.

Anyway, in the summer of 2007, I found that the Venue at Colonial Woods Missionary Church had Saturday night services at 6 pm. Saturday afternoon/evening services are a prerequisite for my attendance because it takes a couple hours to do my morning routine. So I attend Catholic mass at St. Stephen's at 4 pm on Saturday and then my dad and I go to the Venue at 6 pm.

A Changed Man

In 2008, while speaking to Gordie's classes, I noticed a profound change in him. Rather than acting uncomfortable about my faith, he was encouraging me to share and asking me questions. Apparently, earlier in the year he had given his life to Christ and experienced the rebirth. He reports that he had listened to my story many times for several years and merely heard it as a story about destructive-decision making. After all, that's what it had been titled for guest speaking purposes. One day, while I was speaking, it clicked – mine wasn't just a story about a destructive decision; it was a story of redemption.

Gordie said that despite the fact that I had lost most aspects of my health, there was something he saw in me that he knew in his

210

healthy condition, was lacking. That something was faith. It was a genuine relationship with God. He began to pray for a relationship with God like I had. He said that the faith he saw at work in my life inspired him to seek Christ. In 2008, he and has family switched churches and God continued working on his heart. He said that his prayers had been answered at last, that he finally knew what it was like to have a relationship with Christ versus just attending church and going through the motions with various religious rituals. I planted the seed, while his new church family watered it with discipleship. *"So then neither he who plants is anything, nor he who waters, but God who gives the increase. Now he who plants and he who waters are one, and each one will receive his own reward according to his own labor."* (1 Corinthians 3:7-8 NKJV)

God had called Gordie to be a health teacher and now that he was beginning to see things more clearly, he was able to fill in an important dimension of his teaching that had been missing; spiritual health. He realized that we are tripartite beings, made up of body, soul and spirit. In fact, I want to share a communiqué between Gordie and myself that took place after a presentation in December of 2009.

Gordie wrote;

"We were talking about spirituality today in my ELA 1 class and I referred to spirituality as a component of our being or health. I explained that we are comprised of physical, mental, social, and spiritual aspects. I had shared with my class that most of my life I was strong in the first three but spiritually weak. I also referred to how you had lost your physical well-being but became spiritually strong. We debated on what you would rather have; physical or spiritual strength if you could only have one. So I told the class that

I would ask you what you would choose. If you don't mind, can you please answer that question for us?"

I replied;

"Without a doubt spiritual strength is the greater! I was physically strong before the accident, but I was spiritually restless. I had no peace, I was self-destructing! When all you have is physical strength, you're stuck under the illusion that you can do it yourself, you can be god, you have control, that you're healthy (see Matthew 9:12). You're blinded by your own strength!

To keep me from becoming conceited because of these surpassingly great revelations, there was given me a thorn in my flesh, a messenger of Satan, to torment me. Three times I pleaded with the Lord to take it away from me. But he said to me, 'My grace is sufficient for you, for my power is made perfect in weakness.' Therefore I will boast all the more gladly about my weaknesses, so that Christ's power may rest on me. That is why, for Christ's sake, I delight in weaknesses, in insults, in hardships, in persecutions, in difficulties. **For when I am weak, then I am strong."** *(2 Corinthians 12:7-10 NIV* **emphasis added)**

Girlfriend

Laura, a Canadian girl that I had dated briefly in 2006, had left me to pursue a relationship with a former boyfriend of hers. She gingerly stepped back into my life at the beginning of 2009. She was a beautiful young lady, about 5'8" in height with curly brown hair and green eyes that were blue when I first met her. She worked as a nurse in Sarnia. The relationship with her former boyfriend didn't work out. Realizing that she had hurt me in the past, we began not where we left off, but in a new place of friendship. Eventually, she asked if I just wanted to remain friends or embark on a relationship which would result in eventual marriage. She didn't say all that, but knowing how forward looking she was, it was implied.

I had learned to take such decisions to God in prayer, so I told her I'd pray on it. But I was praying after I had already made up my mind; I was definitely interested in a relationship with her. I was seeking God's approval, but what I got instead was His direction. He had impressed heavily upon my heart that I was not to engage Laura in a relationship, beyond friendship.

However, as I said, I had already made up my mind. I'd choose to rebel against what I knew was God's direction. I would mislead Laura into thinking we'd eventually marry, despite the fact that I knew we weren't meant for each other. It made it easier knowing that I was her rebound guy. So as I pursued a relationship with her, I put God's direction out of my mind.

Despite the fact that I was deliberately disobeying what I felt were explicit directions from the Lord, my relationship with Laura was overall most enjoyable. I wouldn't change much of it at all, except for how it ended.

In early May of 2009, we went with my parents to a Paradisus all-inclusive resort in Punta Cana, Dominican Republic. Laura and I shared the same conviction that sex was something sacred to be enjoyed only in a marriage relationship. Even though I had failed in this area earlier in my life, I repented and was determined to keep myself for my wife. Therefore, we had different rooms. Laura shared a room with my mom, and I with my dad.

Not long after we returned from the Dominican Republic, we decided to go out to dinner on our own. Laura had a blue 2001 Toyota Echo, that she nicknamed Elliot. Elliot was very easy to transfer in and out of. We had an enjoyable dinner at Chili's. That was the first of many special outings we shared.

I first met Laura's family when we were dating in 06. She had invited my parents and I to watch a play at Victoria Petrolia Playhouse in Petrolia, Ontario. Two of her younger sisters were in the play. Unfortunately, my mom had become sick, so only my dad and I were able to make it. After the play, her family had us over to their house for dinner. I immediately clicked with her family. I absolutely adored them and romanticized being one of them. That trip was actually the first time I'd been back to Canada since the crash.

Anyway, Laura and I now made several trips to visit her family. On one occasion, I went with Laura to her maternal grandparents' anniversary party. We went out to dinner and the movies a lot, there was a nature trail we often enjoyed, and we just enjoyed one another's company. We had been going to Canada so much that I decided to apply for a Nexus Pass, which would grant us faster access by allowing me to bypass a lot of the customs enforcement.

Meanwhile, it had become quite obvious that Laura had fallen deeply in love with me. If indeed I was once just her bounce-back-boy, someone with whom she could prove to herself that she was lovable, I wasn't any longer. That had changed. When I began to realize this, the memory of God's direction began to move from the back of my mind, where I had thrust it, to the forefront. Along with this recognition of God's direction came a fear that there would be no one else who would have me.

So I wrestled with a feeling that I needed to break up with Laura and a fear that I needed to hang on to her tightly. Ultimately, the fear won out. I doubled down on my rebellion, and as a result I developed an anxiety disorder that still haunts me to this day. To be clear, this did not come from God. 2 Timothy 1:7 states; *"For God has not given us a spirit of fear, but of power and of love and of a sound mind."*

(NKJV) Rather, as a result of my sin of disobedience, the devil gained a foothold in my soul and produced a spirit of fear. (cf. Ephesians 4:27)

One afternoon, without going into details, I shared with Laura that I was having anxiety about our relationship. She didn't understand why I was anxious. Heck, even I didn't fully understand, but I knew that it was connected to the spiritual realm and was a result of my disobedience. However, I did not share any of this with her. Regardless, I don't think my revelation brought an end to our relationship, but rather it brought to the forefront issues that would be a problem later.

Eventually, she decided that she'd be more secure with a man who was more able bodied. She wanted to remain friends, but I decided that any more of this would be pointless and painful. When our relationship ended in the summer of 2009, I made sure that it was final. I wouldn't let her hurt me again, nor would I permit myself to hurt her. I received my Nexus Pass and only had the opportunity to use it once before we broke up. I could have saved myself a lot of pain and anxiety had I heeded God's direction.

Concerning a committed relationship with a woman, I am trusting God with this. If He has someone for me, then He will bring her into my life. I must not force things, and I must not worry about such things. Rather, I need to live in complete surrender, knowing that God is for me (c.f. Romans 8:31).

School's Out (for me, for now)

After the fall semester of 2009, I graduated from the University of Michigan-Flint with a Bachelor of Arts in Psychology. I graduated with highest honors, Suma cum laude, because I had carried a 4.0 grade point average throughout my collegiate career at U of M. But I didn't walk with the graduating class. Instead, I went with my parents and some friends on vacation at an all-inclusive resort in Playa del Carmen, Mexico.

By the time I graduated with my Bachelor's degree, having read and studied the entire Bible, from Genesis to Revelation, numerous times, as well as many other biblical theology centered books, I had a pretty firm grip on theology. So other than adding to my credibility, I really didn't see any purpose in attending a seminary. Although, I do think it would be nice to learn Greek and Hebrew so that I could read the Bible in its original form.

Interview

In January of 2010, I was invited to do a television interview at Northgate Bible Church. The broadcast was called *"God's Intervention Story"* and it aired on local cable access television in February. I remember the interview vividly, because oddly, I was more nervous speaking in front of a television camera than I had ever been speaking to groups of people. Just prior to the interview, Pastor Dave, who conducted the interview, asked what church I attended. I said "Colonial Woods," not realizing that during the interview, Pastor Dave would say that I was a member of Colonial Woods. It wasn't visible on camera, but I felt my face flush when he said this. I wasn't a member and I had neglected to tell him that I also attended St. Stephan's with my parents.

I wanted to jump in and correct him, but my nerves wouldn't allow me, so I just sat there wearing the same silly smile I'd been sporting throughout the interview. When the moment passed, I wasn't too concerned with being called a member of Colonial Woods. However, I was disappointed that I didn't jump in and say, "I also attend St. Stephan's." Sure enough, after the interview, my dad also let me know that he was disappointed that I hadn't mentioned it. I was hit with a flood of anxiety. I had to do whatever possible to correct my omission.

I contacted Kim, who had initially contacted me about the interview. I explained that I had failed to mention that I also attended St. Stephan's Church. I asked if during the part in question, she could create a caption reading, "Ryan also attends St. Stephen's with his parents." She assured me that she could and would. Despite this, the anxiety didn't recede until the program was aired.

Largest Audience

On Thursday, November 11th of 2010, I spoke to around 500 students at Port Huron Northern in their performing arts center. This was the largest crowd I'd spoken to. For the first time, Gordie and I prayed together before the presentation. The prayer was answered. I brought my A game and the response was overwhelming. But Gordie got in trouble with administration because so many students had skipped class to hear the presentation. He had to go through a mad scramble to write passes for those who had requested them.

Concert

The next evening, my friend Scott had hooked me up with VIP tickets to the *"Fly Me to the Show"* tour, featuring Hawk Nelson, Brit Nicole and John Reuben. This was such a blessing because I didn't even really know Scott when he chose to show this kindness. Up until then, I saw him at various concerts in town that I attended.

During the concert, Britt Nicole put her microphone down, came down off the stage, gave me a hug and asked me my name. The concert was so loud that I was sure she hadn't heard me. But afterwards I met her and she said, "Ryan, right?" I got an autograph from and a picture with her. I was also able to give her a website invitation, though I am unsure whether she ever had an opportunity to visit my site. That night, for the first time in my life, I left with a legitimate crush on a pop star.

Youth Pastor for a Night

On Friday night, November 19th of the same year, I spoke to the youth group at Gordie's church – Community Wesleyan in Marysville. My mom didn't go with and since I didn't feel up to giving the presentation alone, I switched it up. I spoke on physical strength versus spiritual strength, by drawing on Samson and King David as examples in contrasts exhibiting these attributes.

Here's a very abbreviated version of my teaching that night; After Delilah's constant nagging, Samson told her *"No razor has ever come on my head; for I have been a Nazirite to God from my mother's womb. If I am shaved, then my strength will go from me, and I will become weak, and be like any other man." (Judges 16:17 WEB)* The Lord is conspicuously absent from Samson's assessment of his strength. In contrast, David wrote, *"**The LORD is my strength** and my shield; My heart trusted in Him, and I am helped." (Psalm 28:7a NKJV **emphasis added**)* David rightly acknowledged the Lord as his strength. Samson exemplifies physical strength, while David exemplifies spiritual strength.

In hindsight, I should have involved more group participation. While not using the language above, (I didn't say "conspicuously," "assessment," or "exemplifies"), I still taught the kids, mostly teenagers, like they were adults, who had their Bibles open. I should have engaged them, asking if they'd ever heard the story of Samson and Delilah, or King David and one of his great exploits, drawing them along with, rather than just speaking to them. I had to chalk it up as a learning experience. Something I'll be better prepared for in the future.

Uncle Bob

I spent the coldest two months of 2010, February and March, with my parents in Florida. While there, my mom mentioned that I was writing a book. So my Great-Uncle Bob, who calls me "the kid," says, "Hey kid! Am I in your book?" I jokingly replied, "Am I in your will?" Every time I see my Uncle Bob, I rightly expect the question, "Am I in the book?" Well, Uncle Bob, now you're in my book. I appreciate your loving encouragement and sense of humor.

Horseback Riding

On Thursday, May 5th 2011, I went horseback riding for the first time in my life. The opportunity to ride a horse is something I thought I had forfeited. Under the instruction of Sue, the owner of Rattle Run Stables, and her daughter Sarah, I began riding at Liberty Riders, for therapeutic purposes. It helped with my balance and core strength, as well as my psychological health (i.e. it's good for the mind). The horse I rode that summer was a blanket Appaloosa named Tony. Tony was an extremely steady horse, who it seemed never got spooked. He reminded me of Eeyore from Winnie the Pooh, just kind of ho-hum.

The next year I began riding an almond brown Quarter Horse named Siege. Siege was a handsome horse, his forelock hung low near his eyes, like a skater punk. It wasn't much longer after Sarah got married that she got pregnant, so Sue entrusted me to Kristen, who has been instructing me since 2013.

"More Head Trauma"

In 2012, I wrote the following in response to some photos I posted on Facebook, in an album titled *"More Head Trauma."* In the photos, I had surgical gauze wrapped around my head with my right eye nearly swollen shut, surrounded with black and purple bruising, as well as some bruising under my left eye. The incident happened in Florida on Monday, March 19th. Below is a copy of what I wrote in my journal, then transferred to a note in Facebook, also titled *"More Head Trauma."*

I would love to write about something cool that happened that caused my recent injuries, but it would be a total fabrication, a lie. Here's what happened; at the place down here in Florida I use a different power chair. We have a portable ramp we use on the front door for my entering and exiting the house.

I had just returned from the gym and my dad switched me from my manual chair that I take to the gym to my power chair. Well, I forgot my seat belt and so did he. He usually buckles it for me. But I had distracted him because I had to use the bathroom immediately after I changed chairs. So I rolled out of the front door and no sooner did I hit the ramp than I quickly slid out of the chair. As soon as my feet hit the ramp, I stood and fell forward. My dad was right behind me and made an unsuccessful attempt to grab me.

I had fallen to the right, directly into this white bricked planter that runs adjacent to the ramp. I'm 6-foot-tall, the ramp is probably about 3 feet at the top, from which the slope is immediate. Add to that the momentum from the slide and the forward fall, which I broke with my head, and my head split wide open. My dad was immediately on top of me, cradling my head, crying "Oh God help us…Oh Jesus help us!" Then he screamed for help for the neighbors to call 911. He looks at me with tears in his eyes and says, "I'm so sorry Ryan!" I was conscious the whole time and I was like, "Dad, calm down, I'm fine." He said, "No Ryan you're not fine." At that point, I looked over my right shoulder and saw that I was lying in a pool of blood. Still, I felt no pain and I felt fine so I continued to try to calm my dad down. The neighbor grabbed a towel and gave it to my dad to compress the wound. I guess the fall had caused a laceration across the top of my forehead about 5 inches long, so that my dad could actually see my skull.

Afterward, I told my dad that it was kind of ironic that I was trying to calm him down, to which he replied, 'You didn't see what I saw!' Anyway, the EMS rushed me to the local hospital, from which they straightaway transported me via helicopter to a hospital in Lakeland that had a trauma unit. Still feeling fine, I was being my witty self with all the ER staff, cracking wise and just making the best. I had a peace about me. I am ready to die whenever, but God wasn't ready for me yet. They ran a CT Scan on me and put 16 stitches on the outside of my forehead and several more on the inside. The CT Scan came back showing no immediate issues and I hadn't displayed any concussion-like symptoms, so they then gave my parents instructions on how to care for the wound, cover and wrap it. I was released at approximately 9:30 pm, and the accident happened at 4:30 in the afternoon. So no matter how it sounds from my account, it did not happen quickly.

I'm gonna have a wicked scar on my forehead, but God is with me. It could have and probably should have been much worse. I could've broken my neck and died, or fallen on my mouth and wrecked my beautiful smile. It's ironic that after being relatively unscarred from the car crash, now, 13 years later, I'm going to have a scar from a separate accident.

There are some humorous things that happened during this ordeal that I can look back and laugh at. Anyone who knows my dad knows that he can't hear well. While the EMS were about to pick me up off the pavement and put me on the stretcher, my dad asked me how I was. I replied "I'm fine." He says, "You're blind?!" He was dead serious!

While I was waiting to be stitched up, my dad came in the room, well he'd been in the room, but he came close to my head and said, "Oh my God!" Startled, I replied, "What?!" At that point my wound opened up and started shooting blood in intervals. My dad said it was like a squirt gun. After that, I told my dad to please leave the room.

After surgery my parents came back into the room, and I told them that I saw "the light." My mom said, "You did?!" To which I replied, "Yeah, they had it above me the whole time they were stitching me up!"

The day after my mishap, my friend Bobbie took a spill of her own. Bobbie was immediately down at our place after my mishap. Bobbie took a misstep off a curb and did a face plant in the middle of the street, breaking her cheek bone. She spent two days in the hospital, while I was released the day of. Before I had seen her, with tongue-in-cheek, I accused her of trying to upstage me. Something I really didn't think was possible. She was released Thursday night and posted on my Facebook wall. What follows is our brief exchange;

Bobbie: "Hey Ryan, I am home now. Bet I am prettier than you. Lol"

Me: "yay! I don't know why you had to go and try and show me up! I'm to see the surgeon tomorrow morning at 11. I heard you were transported to Tampa, they took me to Lakeland. I'll have to stop by tomorrow afternoon so we can compare battle scars."

Bobbie: "You got that right. I bet mine are worse than yours. You just have a bad eye and a band around your head. I have a bad eye and blue, red and green all the way down my neck. Lol. See ya tomorrow."

Me: "ah, but the band around my head's holding my brain in…I kid I kid, but it is covering up what's likely gonna be a nasty scar. Betcha I lost more blood than you!" ☺

Bobbie: "I wouldn't bet on it…"

Several days after the incident, again writing in my journal:

I went and got my stitches out today, Friday, March 23rd. The surgeon, a big burly black man, with a nice white grin, and wisps of hair under his chin, was initially reticent to allow the nurse to remove them. He said that one more day would be optimal, but the weekend was coming and if stitches are in too long they leave railroad tracks. The Doctor looks at me

223

and asks, "What do think?" I replied, "I don't know man, you've got the degree." Smiling, he replied, "So you're going to put this all on me?" He took a close look at the wound, said that it was healing well and gave the okay for the nurse to remove them. After she removed them, the nurse placed butterfly bandages over top. So I can't really see much of the scar, but what I can see doesn't look all that bad.

I had gathered that the surgeon had a good sense of humor and an appreciation for the like. So I gave him a copy of my entry from Monday, which he read right there, chuckling. He then left, making sure to grab his copy.

That afternoon I went down to see Bobbie. She was right, her injuries were far worse than mine. The right side of her face was swollen with all kinds of injury colors; black, blue, purple, green and yellow. Her eyeball was completely blood red. I told her that she won the worst injured prize. We had our picture taken. My mom saw it later that evening and commented that it looked as if we were dressed for Halloween.

Baccalaureate

On June 2nd 2013, I was blessed with the opportunity to speak at the Port Huron area baccalaureate. It had been coordinated by my friend Gordie. I wrote a speech that Gordie transferred to a power point display, so that the audience could follow along without my speech impairment being a hindrance.

Gordie gave me the following introduction, which was much more than I had ever expected. Once again, it was honoring and humbling to realize that God was using me to impact others with the Gospel.

It is my pleasure to introduce our first speaker today, Ryan Krafft. When I was first asked to take on the responsibility of Baccalaureate and I realized I would have to line up speakers for the event, Ryan's name was the first one that popped into my head. Ryan has spoken to my health classes and various other classes in the district for over eight years. I did a little math and figured he has spoken to over 5,000 students in our district. Although his story may focus on the drinking and driving tragedy he was involved in, that left him bound to a wheelchair, Ryan makes it clear that he is only alive today because of his relationship with Jesus Christ. Not only has he been an encouragement for students to make better choices, he has been instrumental in leading many in this district to Christ. I know this because I am one of them. When Ryan first started speaking to my classes I attended church, but I would not say I was a follower of Christ. Despite his physical limitations, I knew Ryan had something in his life that I was missing. That something was Jesus. Not only do I want to thank Ryan for coming here to speak today, but I would like to thank you for changing my life.

Below are the talking points from my speech that the audience could see on PowerPoint above me.

Compromise Leads to Mediocrity

- In order to fit in, all too often we compromise our values and by doing so, we embrace mediocrity (the ordinary).
- This isn't about me, but before the car crash, before I got saved, I was living a life of compromise. I was afraid to stand

out, afraid to be different. Since I embraced compromise, I became mediocre.

- So I know what it's like to be mediocre because of compromise. I'm not referring to compromise in a general sense, which is the settling of a difference by mutual concessions. Compromise in a general sense is often necessary. I'm talking about compromising our values in order to fit in. Compromise of character will lead to a mediocre life.

- When we compromise our values to be more likable or to just get along, we end up destroying our testimony. When we claim to be Christians, but aren't living a life that honors Christ, we dishonor Christ. We take His name in vain.

- I'm not talking about perfection. God knows I'm a mess, I still screw up, I still sin. I'm referring to a life of integrity. Empowered by the Holy Spirit, we're called to pursue a life that consistently strives toward a standard that the world cannot appreciate or accept. We ought to be so genuine that when we fail to live up to who we are in Christ, we confess our fault, shake it off and get back up.

- Our society celebrates sin, and unfortunately, most in the church have compromised. Nowadays, all too often, one can't see a lifestyle difference between a Christian and an atheist. If our talk and our walk don't agree, our testimony will not amount to much. When nonbelievers see nothing different in our lives, they rightly wonder if our profession of faith is sincere. This is what they see; *"They claim to know God, but by their actions they deny him." (Titus 1:16 NIV)*

- The early church stood out – they were counter-culture revolutionaries. *"They think it strange that you do not plunge with them into the same flood of dissipation, and they heap abuse on you." (1 Peter 4:4 NIV)* The early church was thought of as strange, because they didn't run with the crowd! They were charged with having *"turned the world upside down." (Acts 17:6 NKJV)*

Chosen and Called to Shine

- Like the early church, God has redeemed, chosen and called us out of mediocrity. We are called to be extraordinary! We are called to stand out! To be noticed! To be unashamedly different!

- *"You are the light of the world. A city on a hill cannot be hidden. Neither do people light a lamp and put it under a bowl. Instead they put it on its stand, and it gives light to everyone in the house. In the same way,* **let your light shine before men***, that they may see your good deeds and praise your Father in heaven. (Matthew 15:14-16 NIV* **emphasis added***)*

- *"...in which you* **shine like stars** *in the universe as you hold out the word of life." (Philippians 2:15-16 NIV* **emphasis added***)*

- This does not mean that we can't be fashionable, it's our life, rather than our appearance that the world should notice.

- I don't want to downplay the importance of verbally preaching the gospel. Indeed, we are called to preach the Gospel with our words. But as I touched on earlier, if our walk doesn't match our talk, the Gospel will come across as empty and powerless.

- People will want to know your testimony. How has the Gospel changed you? God has given us power to influence one another. Changed lives change lives!
- Seniors, when you leave here today, you will be released into a dark world. You can choose to blend in and contribute to the darkness, or you can let your light shine. My advice to you is Stand Out! Be Extraordinary! Shine!
- Remember you are not only representing your school, your community and your family. You're repping (representing) Christ.

As you might be able to tell, I borrowed from what I had already written in **Becoming.** After the speech, I received a standing ovation.

Kevin

On May 26th 2014, Memorial Day, one of my best friends, Kevin, was killed. Kevin was hit, or more than likely clipped by a car, from behind, while riding his bicycle. The driver of the vehicle, a 32 year old man, was understandably shaken to his core at what had just transpired. So he initially left the scene of the accident, before collecting himself and returning.

Kevin was an exceptional man of great character and a devoted follower of Christ. He was a loving husband, father and grandfather, who doted on his grandchildren. He had been actively involved with Youth for Christ (YFC) since high school, serving as part-time staff person in college and later on the board for the organization. In 2002, the opportunity arose for Kevin to enter into full time ministry with YFC. Anyone who knew Kevin knew that this was his calling.

In his role as a youth director for YFC, he served in Military Community Youth Ministries (MCYM) at Selfridge Air National Guard base, located in Harrison Township. While at Selfridge, Kevin started a "Club Beyond" group. This club was designed to minister to Christian youth on the base and enable them to pray for and spread the Gospel to their peers. Kevin invited me down, and I shared my testimony with the Club Beyond students once.

After ten years, the Executive Director of YFC East Michigan was promoted. While the organization searched for a replacement, Kevin fulfilled all the duties of director for over a year before being promoted to Executive Director. He served in this position for only ten months before being called home to heaven.

You may recall that earlier in my writing I had mentioned Kevin and his wife, Marcia, in regards to our traveling to Georgia for the *"Be in Health"* conference. Kevin made an impact on a lot of people, including me. Before the crash, Kevin and Marcia were just neighbors who lived two houses away. After my rebirth, as brothers in the Lord, Kevin and I clicked. Both of us having similar struggles with anxiety and depression, we were a great help to one another. Kevin would make a point to stop by almost every week, and we'd just talk through things. I truly miss those visits.

Kevin's story didn't stop with his death. In fact, his legacy continued in a beautiful way through his family's testimony of forgiveness. Almost eleven months after the accident, with the blessing of her son Shannon, Marcia, her daughter Stephanie, son-in-law Matt, and the man responsible for Kevin's death, stood before the judge. There, Marcia pleaded for leniency on his behalf, reading this statement; "We, the Collins family, forgive Nathan for whatever his part was in the accident that took Kevin's life and for fleeing the accident scene. To the honorable judge, the Kevin Collins family, without reservation, asks you to grant leniency to Mr. Nathan."

Nathan had already pleaded guilty to failure to stop at the scene of an accident resulting in death, a five-year felony. He also pleaded guilty for driving without insurance, a one-year misdemeanor. Nathan was shown great mercy in that he was sentenced to only 18-months of probation.

As I was speaking with Marcia, who had purposed in her heart to forgive the driver before knowing the circumstances, she revealed that she was able to reason that it was an accident. A harsh sentence wouldn't have taught Nathan anything, neither right nor wrong. She sees God's hands in this, and she even believes that He was preparing her for this.

Watching Marcia cope with losing her husband, whom she so loved, has been remarkable. She truly harbors no anger or unforgiveness, but trusts in God completely. I can only step back and marvel, as I think to myself, *"That's what faith can do!"* The Collins' family truly exemplifies a Colossians 3:13 attitude, *"Bearing with one another, and forgiving each other, if any man has a complaint against any; even as Christ forgave you, so you also do." (WEB)*

Love vs. Tolerance

(I wrote the following in early 2014, after the A&E television
network threatened to suspend Duck Dynasty's Phil Robertson in
December 2013 for expressing the biblical view of homosexuality in
an interview with GQ magazine. The dustup got me thinking of
what role tolerance should play in the Christian life, when often
what we are told to tolerate is contrary to the Christian worldview.
The relevance of this topic took on added significance after the
Supreme Court of the United States redefined marriage to include
same-sex couples on June 26th 2015. In response to this ruling, I
took a stand for traditional marriage on Facebook and received a
barrage of criticism and ridicule.)

A QUOTE FROM Rick Warren reads, "Our culture has
accepted two huge lies. The first is that if you disagree with
someone's lifestyle, you must fear or hate them. The second is that
to love someone means you agree with everything they believe or
do. Both are nonsense. You don't have to compromise convictions
to be compassionate."[31]

This article will focus on the second lie, with the premise being
that loving someone sometimes makes it imperative not only that we
disagree with, but express intolerance towards certain things they
believe and/or do.

Society today has exalted tolerance as a virtue. Scott Scruggs writes "By definition, the function of tolerance is relegated to the social arena in order to protect moral issues, not enforce them. As a result, talking about tolerance as a moral virtue is a circular argument."[32] Nevertheless, tolerance has become the chief moral virtue amongst secularists, while the real chief virtue of love has been sacrificed on the altar of tolerance, for love by definition, must at times be intolerant. Love always wants the best for the beloved; therefore, intolerance is actually an imperative part of love. Love cannot tolerate, condone, approve of, or accept destructive behavior of the beloved. Love may tolerate destructive behavior in the sense that it endures it in order to maintain a relationship with the beloved. But, while respecting the free agency of the beloved, love never truly tolerates the behavior, in the sense of taking a permissive attitude towards destructive behavior.

To do so, may in fact, be the complete opposite of love. Hatred or dislike for an individual is completely tolerant towards behavior that will lead to the eventual destruction of the hated. Or put more succinctly, tolerance of all behavior is the opposite of love – it condones what destroys. Indifference, unlike love or hatred, has no feelings whatsoever for the individual and therefore would display apathy towards all behavior; good, bad, or destructive.

For example, I have a friend who struggles with alcoholism. I do not permit him to drink or be drunk around me. But I endure with him and try to assist him in his fight against this demon. I do not look at him as an alcoholic; I look at him as my friend. Another example; a member of my family has anger issues and he complains almost incessantly, or so it seems at times. This situation is slightly different than the previous example. For instance, to be around him, I have no choice but to permit his angry outbursts and complaining.

232

But I do not condone or approve of these behaviors, and I let him know it.

A common excuse for behavior nowadays is that the individual was born that way and therefore cannot change his or her behavior. In the first example above, it is true that people may have a predisposition towards alcoholism. But to say that they are forever enslaved to the behavior of overdrinking belies reality, as there are a great number of recovering alcoholics among us. In the second example, hypothetically, my family member might say that he's been angry for as far back as he can remember. Therefore, he must have been born angry. This excuse, however, would be shallow and few would argue that his behavior could not be changed.

I make no secret of the fact that I am a born again Christian, and as such, I subscribe to a Christian worldview. So it ought to go without saying that I adhere to the Christian ethic found in the Bible. In Matthew 22:36, Jesus was asked which was the greatest commandment. His response is recorded in Matthew 22:37-40; *"'You shall love the Lord your God with all your heart, with all your soul, and with all your mind.' This is the first and great commandment. A second likewise is this, 'You shall love your neighbor as yourself.' The whole law and the prophets depend on these two commandments."* (WEB) The apostle John explains *"...he who doesn't love his brother whom he has seen, how can he love God whom he has not seen?"* (1 John 4:20 WEB)

Therefore, it is imperative that we, as Christians, love our fellow man, and one way that we express this love is by demonstrating concern, and even intolerance for what our biblical worldview describes as destructive behavior.

The Judeo-Christian standard of morality, being a reflection of an absolutely holy God, is so high that it renders all mankind as sinful. *"For all have sinned and fall short of the glory of God."* (Romans 3:23

ESV) Indeed, we are natural-born sinners. For the Christian, with the realization that eternity awaits all, the most loving thing that we can do is to point others to the need of the Savior, which includes calling sin sinful. You can't receive the cure until you realize that you are sick. Jesus responded to the Pharisees who were questioning him for hanging out with sinners, *"Those who are well have no need of a physician, but those who are sick...For I did not come to call the righteous, but sinners, to repentance." (Mathew 9:12-13 NKJV)* Jesus was not conceding that they were in fact righteous, but the fact that they perceived themselves as such, rendered them beyond healing. "Those who suppose their souls to be without disease will not welcome the spiritual Physician."[33] (Matthew Henry)

Some say that we should not judge. Yet this statement itself is usually issued as a judgment. Indeed, even now, you are judging me according to what I have written and I expect it and willingly accept it. Or else, I would not have written. Rather than a blanket statement about judging, the Christian ethic warns believers against hypocritical judgment. *"For with whatever judgment you judge, you will be judged; and with whatever measure you measure, it will be measured to you." (Matthew 7:2 WEB) "You hypocrite! First remove the beam out of your own eye, and then you can see clearly to remove the speck out of your brother's eye." (Matthew 7:5 WEB)* Also see Romans 2:21-23. So according to Scripture, we are called first and foremost to be intolerant toward our own sinful behavior. Nevertheless, Jesus encouraged proper judgment, *"Don't judge according to appearance, but judge with righteous judgment." (John 7:24 WEB)*

The Christian faith is predicated on the fact that Christ changes people and behavior change follows this experience. This experience is called being *born again* (John 3:3), wherein the believer becomes *a new creation* (2 Corinthians 5:17). New ideals and convictions arise, which lead to behavior change. The Christian call is one of repentance. Repentance can rightly be defined as a change of mind that results in a change of direction or behavior. This call to repent is not a one-time deal. It is an ongoing reality through which a Christian grows and becomes who he is in Christ.

The best way to confront sin is to exalt the word of God; *"For the word of God is living and powerful, and sharper than any two-edged sword, piercing even to the division of soul and spirit, and of joints and marrow, and is a discerner of the thoughts and intents of the heart." (Hebrews 4:12 NKJV)*

This is what Duck Dynasty's Phil Robertson did, however ineloquently. During his interview with GQ, Robertson tried to quote 1 Corinthians 6:9-10 from memory. Written by the apostle Paul, this passage reads; *"Do you not know that the unrighteous will not inherit the kingdom of God? Do not be deceived. Neither fornicators, nor idolaters, nor adulterers, nor homosexuals, nor sodomites, nor thieves, nor covetous, nor drunkards, nor revilers, nor extortioners will inherit the kingdom of God." (NKJV)*

Myself, I was formerly a fornicator, an idolater, a thief, covetous, and a reviler. But I no longer identify with these. I was changed. My behavior didn't change immediately after being born again. In fact, I sometimes still covet and revile, but I don't identify with these. They are not who I am. You see, after Paul's clear declaration that no fornicators, adulterers or homosexuals will inherit the kingdom of God, we find an extraordinarily encouraging word of truth. He goes on to say, ***"And such were some of you.*** *But you were washed, but you were sanctified, but you were justified in the name of the Lord Jesus and by the Spirit of our God." (1 Corinthians 6:11 NKJV **emphasis added**)* The washing, sanctification, and justification occur before the behavior change. God no longer views us as our sin, but rather in Christ, we are separated from sin. And we are called to live as such. Those of us who identify as Christians have a responsibility to participate with God in becoming who we are in Christ. One way we do this is by walking in the Spirit; that is, being sensitive to God's prompting and leading. *"I say then: **Walk in the Spirit**, and you shall not fulfill the lust of the flesh. For the flesh lusts against the Spirit, and the Spirit against the flesh; and these are contrary to one another, so that you do not do the things that you wish. But if you are led by the Spirit, you are not under the law. Now the works of the flesh are evident, which are: adultery, fornication, uncleanness, lewdness, idolatry, sorcery, hatred, contentions, jealousies, outbursts of wrath, selfish ambitions, dissensions, heresies, envy, murders, drunkenness, revelries, and the like; of which I tell you beforehand, just as I also told you in time past, that those who practice such things will not inherit the kingdom of God. But the fruit of the Spirit is love, joy, peace, longsuffering, kindness, goodness, faithfulness, gentleness, self-control. Against such there is no law. And those who are Christ's have crucified the flesh with its passions and desires. **If we live in the Spirit, let us also walk in the Spirit.** Let us not become conceited, provoking one another, envying one another." (Galatians 5:16-26 NKJV* **emphasis added**)

Sinful behavior is neither unforgivable nor irreversible. Some people feel that once one enters into a sinful lifestyle, he will carry the stain of it all his life and beyond. This is untrue. There is a detergent far more powerful than the stain of sin. It is the blood of our Savior Jesus Christ. The same Bible that declares these behaviors to be sin also tells us, *"...the blood of Jesus Christ His Son cleanses us from all sin."* (1 John 1:7b NKJV) [34]

Depending on how far I choose to go, the following could be an article in and of itself. But since it's tied to the theme and it provides a defense for the premise by diffusing a separate argument, I have chosen to include it within.

In the not too distant past, I had a conversation with a young man on Facebook regarding Phil Robertson. In his first remark, he called Robertson a bigot. A friend of mine and I pointed out that Robertson was quoting the Bible. He then said that maybe that was the problem. Then, in a separate post, perhaps after realizing he was assaulting an ethic, said that he has the right to create his own ethic. With that, I did not respond.

Later it occurred to me that while I respect his right to disagree, the position he took is self-defeating. The position he took is called moral relativism. Without appealing to a standard of morality he was essentially saying, "It's morally wrong to say something is morally wrong." Do you see how contradictory and self-defeating this position is? Also, by calling Robertson a bigot for quoting the Bible, he was exercising intolerance (i.e., acting bigoted) toward Robertson without citing a moral standard, other than himself.

As Scott Scruggs, whom I quoted at the beginning, pointed out in his article *"Truth or Tolerance?"* "Any moral standard necessitates intolerance of anything which violates that standard. Merely using the phrase 'a moral standard of tolerance' is a contradiction in terms." Scruggs then cites the words of S.D. Gaede, "If you are intolerant of someone who is intolerant, then you have necessarily violated your own principles. But if you tolerate those who are intolerant, you keep your principle, but sacrifice your responsibility to the principle."[35]

Moreover, the claims of moral relativism are intrinsically self-contradictory, self-refuting, and/or self-defeating. One example is the statement, "there are no absolutes." This is being put forth as an absolute statement, so it is self-defeating. Similarly, those who argue

237

"there is no truth" are asserting that this statement is true. Therefore, it is self-refuting.

As one of my favorite rappers, Lecrae expresses in his song *"Truth,"* "If what's true for you is true for you and what's true for me is true for me, what if my truth says yours is a lie? Is it still true?"[36]

In my opinion, the idea that one can create his own moral standard ranks up there with the delusion that one can create his own reality. If you create reality, it is no longer reality, but fantasy. True reality is bound to crush individual fantasy, unless one chooses to live in a state of perpetual denial. Similarly, true morality will inevitably bear down on the individual when his true, right or proper sense of morality is violated, and/or when he ultimately faces God in judgment (cf. Hebrews 9:27).

At any rate, I hope that I have made it clear that when you call someone intolerant, you yourself are practicing intolerance. Likewise, when you label someone a bigot for a moral stance, you are being bigoted.

Some are bound to accuse me of trying to impose my faith and morality on them, to which I reply, nonsense. I can no more force my belief and morals on you through words than someone can impose their unbelief and immortality on me through the same. Although I'm glad you have, no one has forced you to read this, nor are you required to agree with it. Rather, I am appealing to your conscience and intellect through words, and I'm blessed with the opportunity to influence you.

Nevertheless, I want to end with a clear invitation to embrace the Gospel. As I described earlier, only those who realize they're sick will understand their need for a physician. Only those who realize that they are drowning will see their need for a Savior.

Our sin nature is the great equalizer; the ground is level at the cross. There is no room for pride there. We come as we are, unable to heal ourselves, unable to save ourselves, unable to make ourselves clean or worthy before God. Salvation is typically laid hold of through prayer – a sincere crying out to God to forgive us, heal us, save us, and change us. You can pray with your own words or you can use the prayer which I have provided below from my website www.ryankrafftproject.com

"Lord, forgive me! It was my sin for which you were stripped and whipped. It was my sin that thrust that crown of thorns on your head. *(Can you see it?)* It was my sin that drove those nails into your feet and wrists. *(Can you feel it?)* It was for me you were crucified. I sincerely receive the gift of grace, which you made possible by this act of obedience to the Father. I also sincerely receive the justification, which was made possible by your subsequent resurrection. Lord, come in. Save me now and change me from the inside out. Help me to become a better (wo)man. In Jesus name. Amen. (Don't just read this; meditate on it, speak it, let it become a part of you.)

Physical Assessment

I HAD FINISHED the last chapter, **Expectations,** but after some time, it occurred to me that I wasn't finished with this book. Many are likely interested to know how I am doing physically. I saw the most gains physically within the first 2 or 3 years after the crash. I worked my way up to 175 pounds, only 5-pounds shy of my pre-crash weight, though not nearly as muscular. I actually tended to hover between 170 and 175, usually staying closer to 170.

Erroneously, in my mind I thought that if I could walk, everything else would fall into place. At the expense of other abilities, a primary focus of mine has always been walking. I never progressed to be able to walk without a walker, mainly because I have issues with keeping my balance. This meant that somebody needed to walk behind me to make sure that I didn't fall backward or forward. Nevertheless, I had progressed to a point where I was walking well and near falls rarely happened. I maintained this progress I made, until I began to notice myself slightly regressing. I was slowly losing the gains that I had made.

You may recall what I referred to as "the Chicago lean" in **Home.** It was an uncontrolled lean to the right. Even though I now have control over my core and can correct my posture, over time I developed a tendency to lean to the right. However, in my mind it feels like I'm not leaning. For example, my dad will tell me to sit up straight and my usual reply is "I thought I was."

Well, this lean transferred into my walk and it throws my balance off even more. I still have difficulty holding onto the walker with my right hand. This is most inconsistent, as sometimes I'll have minimal problems, while other times my hand will pitch fits causing major problems with my walk. I walk about a half an hour every day for exercise.

My assessment of my walking is this; I walk like a goon. I am considerably dependent on the walker, hunched over top with my head tending towards the ground, as I can't resist the urge to keep my feet within my lower vision. When it gets real difficult, I drop my head down and look directly at my feet. I also make funny faces, unless a pretty lady comes by, then I'm all smiles. Though the funny faces vary, it's not uncommon for me to walk with my mouth wide open, like I'm trying to catch flies. Fortunately, I haven't caught any. At this point, I'm blessed to still be able to walk.

In July of 2013, the Port Huron Fitness Center closed because Hilton had bought the Thomas Edison Inn, where the Fitness Center was located. Hilton was renovating the Inn, changing it into a DoubleTree Hotel. So that I wouldn't miss my exercise, my dad and I decided to start working out at Anytime Fitness in Marysville. One day, I shared my story with the General Manager, Bobby. I came in two days later, and he had been so inspired by me that he told me he spoke with the owner, who also happened to be his nephew, Jeff. Jeff gave me a lifetime membership. Bobby also gave me a free Anytime Fitness of Marysville T-shirt.

This was a blessing, but I have experienced blessings quite frequently as I walk with the Lord. I already had a lifetime membership to Port Huron Fitness Center. After the renovations were complete, which included updating all the machines, I had an opportunity to choose which gym was better for me. I love the owner of the Port Huron Fitness Center, Karen, like a sister. But Anytime Fitness was much more spacious and the machines were easier for me to use. However, the Port Huron Fitness Center had something that Anytime didn't have; a swimming pool. So I made use of both gyms, working out at Anytime and then shooting over to the Fitness Center to do aquatic therapy. The only time I am able to walk unassisted, with my head up, and come close to my 6-foot height is in the water. Even though I really don't like working out in the pool and would much rather work out on land, I know that the pool is very beneficial for me.

Nevertheless, during my workouts is when my physical regression is most noticeable. I feel as though I stumble from machine to machine, and when there, I am unable to do as much weight as I once did. Even with the free weights on the bench, where I once excelled, there is an increased difficulty, so I had to lower the weight of the free weights. I also lost a considerable amount muscle mass. At a doctor's appointment on January 6th 2015, I weighed in at 155 lbs. That's 21 lbs. loss from around the same time the year before.

On September 23rd, 2015, while working out on the elliptical at Anytime Fitness, I had an excruciating pain in my left leg. I sat down to assess things when my dad noticed that my left leg was swollen. We went to the emergency room, and sure enough, I had a blood clot in my groin on the left side. The ER doctor prescribed Xarelto for six months and set no physical restrictions.

However, since then I have noticed that my left leg has been considerably weaker. There isn't any pain, but it's difficult to lift the thigh. I am almost forced to drag my left leg while walking. A friend of mine later pointed out that leg weakness is a side effect of Xarelto. My primary physician confirmed that I had to stay on Xarelto for six months, and after that, take a whole adult Aspirin daily.

However, I made the switch from Xarelto to Aspirin on March 23rd, 2016 and the leg weakness still persists. Rest assured, I am not complaining. My world is not that small. I know that I'm blessed to be able to do what I do physically. I have met many people and have many disabled friends who would love to have the struggles I have.

Rather than let these struggles get me down, I have allowed them to change my focus. Several Scripture passages have come alive and taken on special meaning for me. I discuss one of these below.

"Therefore we do not lose heart. Even though our outward man is perishing, yet the inward man is being renewed day by day. For our light affliction, which is but for a moment, is working for us a far more exceeding and eternal weight of glory, while we do not look at the things which are seen, but at the things which are not seen. For the things which are seen are temporary, but the things which are not seen are eternal." (2 Corinthians 4:16-18 NKJV)

This passage is one of my favorites. I love personalizing it by replacing the pronouns "we, our, and us," with I, my, and me. For example, *"For **my** affliction, which is but for a moment is working for **me**…"* I'd like to unpack it for you a little bit, to help you understand why this is one of my favorite passages.

Therefore we do not lose heart. The NIV translates *heart* as *"hope."* *"Even though our outward man is perishing,"* that is, even though our bodies are decaying and dying. *"Yet the inward man is being renewed day by day,"* that is, we are growing, being renewed by the grace of God daily. *"For our light affliction,"* in context, the affliction in view here is that of Paul and his companions, which they suffered for Christ's sake. I don't mean to imply that my affliction is in any way equal to theirs. However, as a result of the Fall of Man, everyone bears an affliction; some outwardly, some inwardly. Paul writes that this affliction is light. For believers, our affliction, compared with the physical and spiritual affliction that Christ suffered on our behalf and contrasted with the weight of glory to come, is light. *"Which is but for a moment,"* in light of eternity, which Paul is about to highlight, our affliction is but for a moment. *"Is working for us a far more exceeding and eternal weight of glory."* Here we see Paul's focus begins to shift away from the temporary affliction they were experiencing, to the eternal weight of glory. Rather than fight the affliction, they embraced it and allowed it to work for an eternal glory. Let us do the same, for this is how eternal eyesight is developed. *"While we do not look at the things which are seen, but at the things which are not seen. For the things which are seen are temporary, but the things which are not seen are eternal."*

Not only have I allowed this blessed affliction to enable me to look beyond the temporary to the eternal, it also has given me an eagerness for the return of Jesus. I am eagerly *"looking for the blessed hope and glorious appearing of our great God and Savior Jesus Christ." (Titus 2:13 NKJV)*

The second coming of Jesus is another staple doctrine or principle that is inseparable from biblical Christianity. As Christians, we ought to be preoccupied with the return of Christ. Unfortunately, most Christians in North America are too comfortable in the world and express little eagerness for the return of Christ.

The Bible is clear that the second coming is an integral part of the Christian faith. According to Scripture, our anticipation of this event will affect how we live while in the world. Here's a sampling of some Scripture passages:

"You men of Galilee, why do you stand looking into the sky? This Jesus, who was received up from you into the sky will come back in the same way as you saw him going into the sky." (Acts 1:11 WEB)

"For our citizenship is in heaven, from which we also eagerly wait for the Savior, the Lord Jesus Christ." (Philippians 3:20 NKJV)

"I command you therefore before God and the Lord Jesus Christ, who will judge the living and the dead at his appearing and his Kingdom: preach the word; be urgent in season and out of season; reprove, rebuke, and exhort, with all patience and teaching." (2 Timothy 4:1-2 WEB)

"To those who eagerly wait for Him He will appear a second time, apart from sin, for salvation." (Hebrews 9:28 NKJV)

"Therefore, preparing your minds for action, and being sober-minded, set your hope fully on the grace that will be brought to you at the revelation of Jesus Christ." (1 Peter 1:13 ESV)

Beloved, now we are children of God, and it is not yet revealed what we will be. But we know that, when he is revealed, we will be like him; for we will see him just as he is. Everyone who has this hope set on him purifies himself, even as he is pure." (1 John 3:2-3 WEB)

Expectations

I DON'T ENTERTAIN any illusions, as my expectations are tempered by reality. So what do I expect from this writing? Basically, as I wrote in the **Introduction,** I hope to engage and challenge you. I am truly blessed and honored that you have read my book; I feel privileged to have been able to share with you. However, I know that I cannot convince you of anything, but I pray that you will honestly contemplate what I have written and that God, through His Holy Spirit, will work in your soul and draw you to Himself.

On the real though, Scripture has told me what to expect. As I explained in **Becoming,** the follower of Christ will be mocked, criticized, ridiculed, insulted, hated (John 15:18-19), and persecuted (John 15:20, 2 Timothy 3:12). This is not something that I look forward to, but a reality that I am prepared for because I have clearly explained the Gospel of Jesus Christ. The Gospel is offensive. *"For the message of the cross is foolishness to those who are perishing, but to us who are being saved it is the power of God... Christ crucified, to the Jews a stumbling block and to the Greeks foolishness." (1 Corinthians 18-23 NKJV)*

In today's language, *"the Jew"* can be likened to those who are religious, seeking to attain eternal life through their own merit, and *"the Greek"* can be likened to those who through "learning" and empty philosophy deny the Gospel. God can break through both mindsets! *"But to those who are called, both Jews and Greeks, Christ the power of God and the wisdom of God." (1 Corinthians 1:24 NKJV)* Either way, the Gospel demands that we humble ourselves, admit our sin and our need for a Savior, and accept the gift of salvation that only comes through Jesus Christ. Because I love people and want them to experience this undeserved gift of amazing grace, love and forgiveness through Him, I count it a privilege to bear the reproach of Christ. (cf. Hebrews 11:26; 13:13)

Since I have broken many "sacred cows," some without elaborating, I expect those who are accustomed to "religious thought" to take offense. Their first inclination will be to take the things I've written to their priest, pastor or teacher, and I don't object to that. I just ask that in addition to that, you'd search these things out for yourself. Like the Bereans of Acts 17:11, test everything against the plumb line or standard of Scripture. Then it is up to you whose authority you accept – God's or man's.

I expect some pastors and theologians to pick this book apart. I am open to correction and we can have legitimate disagreements about peripheral issues, but if it's a nonessential, I ask that you'd be gracious towards me.

Similarly, I expect many to dismiss much of what I've written because I don't have any formal theological training. Obviously, I reject the distinction between clergy and laymen as unbiblical. I contend that every follower of Christ has a responsibility to know the Word of God and preach the Gospel.

Nevertheless, I had my friend and theologian, Dr. Todd Baker check the basic theology contained in this book. He wrote back in a conversational email, "Looks great. I like the fact that you go into detail what the Gospel is and what it does for the believer from justification to glorification. You have a good solid understanding of theology."

248

I know of some who will accuse me of putting such a heavy emphasis on the personal reading of Scripture, that I have deemphasized the church community. Although I may not have emphasized church community to meet the liking of some, the Bible reinforces the church community and encourages fellowship. *"Let us not give up meeting together, as some are in the habit of doing, but let us encourage one another—and all the more as you see the Day approaching."* (Hebrews 10:25 NIV) Nor does personal Bible reading make pastors and teachers unnecessary. Indeed, much of what I've written has been learned from such.

Moreover, as I emphasized the need for discernment in **Deception,** becoming more knowledgeable about the Bible will enhance one's ability to discern. In fact, without Scripture reading, it is nearly impossible to discern, because the Bible is the standard by which we ought to judge all things.

I've had many opportunities to put biblical discernment to work. Let me share just one example. I once sat through a sermon, in which after the minister declared in no uncertain terms, his opposition to the biblical doctrine of salvation by grace through faith alone. To bolster his argument, he cherry picked Colossians 1:24; *"Now I rejoice in what was suffered for you, and I fill up in my flesh what is still lacking in regard to Christ's afflictions, for the sake of his body, which is the church."* (NIV) He quoted this verse (Colossians 1:24) without reference or context, in an effort to declare that the sacrifice of Christ is insufficient (*lacking*) for our salvation and that we are to pray, work and suffer *to fill up what is still lacking.*

I immediately realized that he was mishandling Scripture, but I didn't have a copy of the Bible with me and I was in no state to confront him. I was heated, because I'm obviously passionate about the Word of God, and when you lose your cool in an argument, you lose the argument.

When I got home I opened the Scriptures to Colossians 1:24, and as I had suspected, the context completely refuted his argument. If you'll recall in the section **Of Great Consequence,** I referenced that Colossians 1:20 is a verse commonly misused by Christian Universalists. How is it that one group can snatch a verse and claim that everyone and everything is already saved, and yet another group snatches a verse relatively close and claim that no one is saved as of yet, since salvation is incomplete? It's all about context. In our understanding of Scripture, we must not neglect the immediate text around a verse. I have heard it said that text taken out of context leads to pretext. Dictionary.com defines pretext as; "something that is put forward to conceal a true purpose or object."

So let's once again look the context and ferret out the meaning. Here is the passage within its context;

19 "For it pleased the Father that in Him all the fullness should dwell, 20 and by Him to reconcile all things to Himself, by Him, whether things on earth or things in heaven, having made peace through the blood of His cross. 21 And you, who once were alienated and enemies in your mind by wicked works, 22 yet now He has reconciled in the body of His flesh through death, to present you holy, and blameless, and above reproach in His sight— 23 if indeed you continue in the faith, grounded and steadfast, and are not moved away from the hope of the Gospel which you heard, which was preached to every creature under heaven, of which I, Paul, became a minister. 24 I now rejoice in my sufferings for you, and fill up in my flesh what is lacking in the afflictions of Christ, for the sake of His body, which is the church, 25 of which I became a minister according to the stewardship from God which was given to me for you, to fulfill the word of God, 26 the mystery which has been hidden from ages and from generations, but now has been revealed to His saints. 27 To them God willed to make known what are the riches of the glory of this mystery among the Gentiles: which is Christ in you, the hope of glory. 28 Him we preach, warning every man and teaching every man in all wisdom, that we may present every man perfect in Christ Jesus. 29 To this end I also labor, striving according to His working which works in me mightily. (Colossians 1:19-29 NKJV)

First, the apostle Paul writes about the redemptive work of Christ (Colossian 1:19-23). He assures the believers in Colosse that their reconciliation and peace with God were achieved *"through the blood of His cross"* and *"in the body of His flesh through death."* Reconciliation with God it is not achieved through the work and suffering of Christ's ministers. Neither was or is reconciliation brought about by the suffering of His mystical body, the church, but *"in the body of His flesh,"* that is, by the sacrifice of His human physical body and the shedding of His blood. The apostle does not instruct Christians to add something to the work of Christ in order to be reconciled with God. Rather, Paul assures the believers that they are already at peace with Him on account of Christ's blood.

After making the means of reconciliation clear, Paul shifts subjects to his role as an apostle. (cf. Colossians 1:23-29) Immediately following the verse in question, in verse 25 the apostle emphasizes his calling and role as an apostle; *"a minister according to the stewardship from God… to fulfill the word of God."* To fulfill his ministry of making the Gospel known, Paul had to suffer hardship and persecution of every sort.

So exactly *"what is lacking in the afflictions of Christ?"* According to the context, it must be the proclamation of the Gospel. We are redeemed through the blood of Jesus Christ alone. The work and suffering of the apostle Paul, as well as other Christians, serve for

251

the proclamation of the Gospel, not for redemption. Christ is the Redeemer; we are the redeemed, not co-redeemers.

As you can see, if I was not familiar with the Bible, I would not have been able to discern and guard myself against the false teaching that this minister was preaching. This is why it is s critical for every believer to become a student of the Word, so that we can discern and know the truth, rather than believing or being confused by things we hear or read.

In **A Time of Darkness,** I wrote that I would return to the subject of the truth of the finished work and sufficiency of Christ. So I figured that focusing on the sufficiency of the triumph of the crucifixion of Christ would be an appropriate place to end this book. Below is Scriptural evidence, with the letter to the Hebrews being the clearest. A plain reading ought to convince you of the biblical truth behind this argument. As I have throughout this book, I encourage you to look at the context of these Scriptures.

*"When Jesus had received the sour wine, he said, **'It is finished,'** and he bowed his head and gave up his spirit." (John 19:30 ESV **emphasis added**)*

*"For the death that He died, He died to sin **once for all**; but the life that He lives, He lives to God." (Romans 6:10 NKJV **emphasis added**)*

"In whom we have our redemption through his blood, the forgiveness of our trespasses, according to the riches of his grace." (Ephesians 1:7 WEB)

*When you were dead in your sins and in the uncircumcision of your sinful nature, God made you alive with Christ. **He forgave us <u>all</u> our sins**, having canceled the written code, with its regulations, that was against us and that stood* *opposed to us; he took it away, nailing it to the cross. (Colossians 2:13-14 NIV* **emphasis added**)

"…who being the brightness of His glory and the express image of His person, and upholding all things by the word of His power, **when He had by Himself purged our sins**, *sat down at the right hand of the Majesty on high…" (Hebrews 1:3 NKJV* **emphasis added**)

"Unlike the other high priests, he does not need to offer sacrifices day after day, first for his own sins, and then for the sins of the people. **He sacrificed for their sins once for all when he offered himself.***" (Hebrews 7:27 NIV* **emphasis added**)

Through his own blood, entered in **once for all** *into the Holy Place, having obtained eternal redemption." (Hebrews 9:12 WEB* **emphasis added**)

"He then would have had to suffer often since the foundation of the world; but now, once at the end of the ages, He has appeared to put away sin by the sacrifice of Himself. And as it is appointed for men to die once, but after this the judgment, **so Christ was offered once to bear the sins of many.** *To those who eagerly wait for Him He will appear a second time, apart from sin, for salvation." (Hebrews 9:26-28 NKJV* **emphasis added**)

"By which will we have been sanctified through the offering of the body of Jesus Christ **once for all***." (Hebrews 10:10 WEB* **emphasis added**)

"…because by one sacrifice he has made perfect forever those who are being made holy." (Hebrews 10:14 NIV)

*"**Who Himself bore our sins in His own body on the tree**, that we, having died to sins, might live for righteousness—by whose stripes you were healed." (1 Peter 2:24 NKJV* **emphasis added**)

*"**For Christ died for sins once for all**, the righteous for the unrighteous, to bring you to God. He was put to death in the body but made alive by the Spirit…" (1 Peter 3:18 NIV* **emphasis added**)

"…the blood of Jesus Christ, his Son, cleanses us from all sin." (1 John 1:7 WEB)

This is where it's at my friends, the beauty and confidence that comes from knowing the absolute sufficiency of the death and resurrection of Christ. That He has conquered sin and death apart from any help from mankind. The only thing we contributed, if it be called a contribution, was our sin. *"And this is eternal life, that they may know You, the only true God, and Jesus Christ whom You have sent." (John 17:3 NKJV)*

Finally, it is my sincere pray that if you don't or didn't know Christ, you have been exposed to His glory, and as such, you will come to place your complete faith in Him for salvation. That you'd allow Him to change your life, as He has mine. I also pray for my readers who already know, that is, have exercised complete trust in Jesus, that your faith will have been further developed and deepened as you read my story, your story, His story. May you be blessed with an insatiable appetite for God's Word.

Appendix A

This is to the Christian who objects to my use of the law. If the quote at the beginning of the **Bad News in the Mirror** section was insufficient, let me reassure you that it is not my intention to exalt the law above or even equal to the dispensation of Grace, which is far more glorious. Even though the law God gave to Israel contains 613 commandments, I am not lifting up any of these or even the Ten Commandments as a standard that we must keep to obtain righteousness. Indeed, I agree with Paul that righteousness cannot be obtained through the law. *"I don't make void the grace of God. For if righteousness is through the law, then Christ died for nothing!"* (Galatians 2:21 WEB)

Rather, it is my intention to make people aware of their sinful state, apart from Christ. According to Romans 3:20, it is *"through the law* (that) *we become conscious of sin."* (NIV) Indeed, *"the law was put in charge to lead us to Christ that we might be justified by faith."* (Galatians 3:24 NIV)

After Paul declared the law *"holy, righteous and good"* he wrote, *"Did then that which is good become death to me? May it never be!* **But sin, that it might be shown to be sin,** *by working death to me through that which is good***; that through the commandment sin might become exceedingly sinful.***" (Romans 7:13 WEB **emphasis added**)

"But we know that the law is good if one uses it lawfully, knowing this: that the law is not made for a righteous person, but for the lawless and insubordinate, for the ungodly and for sinners, for the unholy and profane, for murderers of fathers and murderers of mothers, for manslayers, for fornicators, for sodomites, for kidnappers, for liars, for perjurers, and if there is any other thing that is contrary to sound doctrine." (1 Timothy 1:8-10 NKJV)

This is the New Testament in which Paul is writing, and yet, the law is still showing the knowledge of sin; it is still being used as a tool to expose sin and immorality. *"The law of the LORD is perfect, converting the soul." (Psalm 19:7 NKJV)*

I do not intend to place anyone in bondage under the law, as I see the purpose of the law is to highlight sin, not to save or even sanctify. I could not find a source of reference for this, but it is said that D.L. Moody said, "The Law can only chase a man to Calvary, no further." I agree with this statement.

According to Scripture, the law is not the only way one is convicted. Jesus, speaking of the Holy Spirit in John 16:8-11, said, *"When he has come, he will convict the world about sin, about righteousness, and about judgment; about sin, because they don't believe in me; about righteousness, because I am going to my Father, and you won't see me anymore; about judgment, because the prince of this world has been judged." (WEB)*

Nevertheless, I would argue that knowledge of and conviction under the law is an appropriate instrument to show a sinner his need for the Savior, and it is for this purpose I make use of the law.

Appendix B

I did not **emphasize** it in the section entitled **Becoming,** where I referred to Hebrews 8:6-13, but you might have noted that in Hebrews 8:8 and 8:10, the Lord is explicit that His covenant was to be with Israel and Judah. Likewise, in the Ezekiel 36:26-27 passage quoted, the context is clearly referring to Israel. *"Therefore say to the house of Israel..." (Ezekiel 36:22 NKJV)*

Regarding Israel, the apostle Paul wrote, *"So I ask, did they stumble in order that they might fall? By no means! Rather through their trespass salvation has come to the Gentiles, so as to make Israel jealous." (Romans 11:11 ESV)* The trespass in this verse refers to Israel's rejection of the Messiah and the principle of salvation by grace. So while some individual Jews are being saved, like Paul himself, national Israel has been temporarily set aside, and Gentile (i.e. non Jewish) believers in Jesus have been blessed to share in the New Covenant with believing Israel.

We are members of Christ's body; *"But you are a chosen people, a royal priesthood, a holy nation, a people belonging to God, that you may declare the praises of him who called you out of darkness into his wonderful light. Once you were not a people, but now you are the people of God; once you had not received mercy, but now you have received mercy." (1 Peter 2:9-10 NIV)* The church is a holy nation made up of many ethnic groups. Therefore, in her, *"There is neither Jew nor Greek, there is neither slave nor free, there is neither male nor female; for you are all one in Christ Jesus." (Galatians 3:28 NKJV)*

The church shares in the New Covenant by way of Christ's blood. *"Therefore, remember that formerly you who are Gentiles by birth and called 'uncircumcised' by those who call themselves 'the circumcision' (that done in the body by the hands of men) — remember that at that time you were separate from Christ, excluded from citizenship in Israel and foreigners to the covenants of the promise, without hope and without God in the world. But now in Christ*

Jesus you who once were far away have been brought near through the blood of Christ." (Ephesians 2:11-13 NIV)

We have been supernaturally grafted into Israel's new covenant relationship with God. (c.f. Romans chapter 11) But for end time purposes, according to my understanding, it's important to make a distinction. The church is not Israel and Israel is not the church. They are two separate entities, with two separate programs, predetermined by God. However, there is naturally some blurring between the two in the Jewish believer. He is a member of the church and of Israel. He is of *"the Israel of God." (Galatians 6:16 NKJV)*

End Notes

[1] Found on internet at http://www.harpercollinschristian.com/permissions/

[2] Charles Leiter, *Justification and Regeneration*, (2007; Hannibal, MS: Granted Ministries Press, 2009)

[3] Dave Hunt, *In Defense of the Faith*, (Eugene, OR: Harvest House Publishers, 1996) p. 172

[4] Melody Green, David Hazard, *No Compromise: The Life Story of Keith Green*, (1989; Nashville, TN: Thomas Nelson, 2008)

[5] Matthew Henry, *Matthew Henry's Commentary*, Text is in public domain, found on internet at http://www.christnotes.org/commentary.php?com=mhc&b=40&c=9

[6] C.S. Lewis, *Mere Christianity*, (1952; New York, NY: HarperCollins Publishers, 2001)

[7] Ibid.

[8] Melody Green and David Hazard, *No Compromise: The Life Story of Keith Green*, (1989; Nashville, TN: Thomas Nelson Publishers, 2008)

[9] C.S. Lewis, *Mere Christianity*, (1952; New York, NY: HarperCollins Publishers, 2001)

[10] Ibid.

[11] Henri Blocher, *Evil and the Cross*, (1994; Grand Rapids, MI: Kregal Publishers, 2004)

[12] Sir William Ramsay, *The Bearing of Recent Discoveries on the Trustworthiness of the New Testament.* Grand Rapids, MI: Baker Book House, 1953, p. 222

[13] Erwin Raphael McManus, *Uprising: A Revolution of the Soul*, (Nashville, TN: Thomas Nelson, 2003)

[14] C.S. Lewis, *The Problem of Pain*, (1940; New York, NY: HarperCollins Publishers, 2001)

[15] John Piper, *Desiring God*, (1986: Colorado Springs, CO: Multnomah Books, 2011) p.226

[16] Patrick Zukeran, *God Wins: A Critique of Rob Bell's Love Wins* Found on the internet at https://www.probe.org/god-wins-a-critique-of-rob-bells-love-wins/

[17] John Piper, *Desiring God*, (1986: Colorado Springs, CO: Multnomah Books, 2011) p.59

[18] Jason Carlson, *Defending Salvation Through Christ Alone;* Paraphrased from article found on the internet at
http://www.christianministriesintl.org/articles/Defending-Salvation-Through-Christ-Alone.php

[19] H. A. Ironside, *An Ironside Expository Commentary; Romans and Galatians,* (1920; Grand Rapids, MI: Kregal Publications, 2006)

[20] John Piper, *Desiring God,* (1986: Colorado Springs, CO: Multnomah Books, 2011) p.227

[21] Neil Anderson, Hal Baumchen, *Finding Hope Again: Overcoming Depression,* (Ventura, CA: Regal Books, 1999)

[22] H. A. Ironside, *An Ironside Expository Commentary; Romans and Galatians,* (1920; Grand Rapids, MI: Kregal Publications, 2006)

[23] William Edward Schenk, *Nearing Home: Comforts and Councils for the Aged,* (Philadelphia: Presbyterian Board of Publication, 1868)

[24] Dave Hunt, *In Defense of the Faith,* (Eugene, OR: Harvest House Publishers, 1996) p. 316

[25] Found on internet at http://www.secretservice.gov/money_detect.shtml

[26] C.S. Lewis, *The Problem of Pain,* (1940; New York, NY: HarperCollins Publishers, 2001)

[27] Ted Dekker, *Adam* Bonus Material, (Nashville, TN: Thomas Nelson, 2008)

[28] *The Usual Suspects,* directed by Bryan Singer (Polygram Filmed Entertainment and Spelling Films International, 1995)

[29] C.S. Lewis, *The Screwtape Letters,* (1942; New York, NY: HarperCollins Publishers, 1996)

[30] I was unable to secure permission from the artist and/or the label to use these lyrics. So I am hoping that my use of them falls under the *fair use doctrine*. Artist; *DC Talk* Album; *Free At Last* Song; *The Hardway* Released in 1992

[31] I was unable to find a source for this quote attributed to Rick Warren

[32] Scott Scruggs, *Truth or Tolerance;* Found on Internet
http://www.probe.org/site/c.fdKEIMNsEoG/b.4224839/k.D58B/Truth_or_Tolerance.htm

[33] Matthew Henry, *Matthew Henry's Commentary,* Text is in public domain, found on internet at http://www.christnotes.org/commentary.php?com=mhc&b=40&c=9

[34] Dennis Pollock, *Responding to Homosexuality;* Found on internet
http://www.sogmin.org/downloads/article_downloads/100-199/133_responding.pdf

[35] Scott Scruggs, *Truth or Tolerance*; Found on Internet
http://www.probe.org/site/c.fdKEIMNsEoG/b.4224839/k.D58B/Truth_or_To
lerance.htm

[36] I was unable to secure the permission of the artist and/or the label to use these lyrics. So I am hoping that my use of them falls under the *fair use doctrine*. Artist; *Lecrae* Album; *Rebel* Song; *Truth* Released in 2008

60043587R00164

Made in the USA
Charleston, SC
22 August 2016